A Lincolnshire Volunteer

The Boer War Letters of Private Walter Barley and Comrades

Cecillie Swaisland

DEDICATED
to the memory of four sisters,
Lenna, Ada, May and Molly,
who, as little girls,
knew and loved Walter Barley
and kept his memory green for the rest of their lives.

First published in 2000 by LITERATIM

Printed in Great Britain by the University of Hull

British Library Cataloguing in Publication Data
A catalogue record for this book is available from the British Library.

ISBN 0 9539754 0 1

Contents

List of Illustrations

The **front cover** shows a detail from Fig. 8. The **back cover** shows the author at the age of three years, with her family, *en route* to South Africa in 1930.

v

Acknowledgements

I am indebted to the following people and institutions for their help and advice during the writing of this book. My thanks go especially to my husband, Charles, for his interest, support and advice. I also remember with love and gratitude the contribution made by my late aunt, May Sergeant, as she recalled events from her childhood and found letters and mementoes of Walter Barley among her possessions. My cousin Thelma Bones and her husband Ted of Scunthorpe helped me to locate facts about Walter's home town.

My thanks to the Central Libraries of Scunthorpe and Hull for access to the local newspapers of the period from which much supporting material was gleaned. Rhodes House Library, University of Oxford, provided useful background information on the South African War. I am particularly grateful to the Museum of Lincolnshire Life, Lincoln, and to Andrew Davies, the Assistant Keeper of Social History, for the opportunity to go through their collection of memorabilia of the Boer War.

In South Africa, the collections of the Cory Library, Rhodes University, Grahamstown, and the Killie Campbell Library, Durban, were of great assistance, as were those of the South African Library, Cape Town. I am grateful to them all.

Finally, thanks are due to A.P. Watt Ltd for granting permission, on behalf of the National Trust for Places of Historic Interest or National Beauty, to quote Rudyard Kipling's verses.

Cecillie Swaisland
Oxford
May 2000

PART ONE

The Background

Chapter 1

Background to the Letters

THE SOUTH AFRICAN WAR

11 October 1899 to 31 May 1902

How much Walter Barley knew about the tensions in South Africa in the years before the outbreak of the South African War is not known. It is clear, however, from mentions in the letters, that families from the north of England who were known to the Volunteers had emigrated there in the later years of the nineteenth century. Although South Africa was not as favoured a destination as the New World or the Antipodes, it had since the 1820s attracted a steady flow of British emigrants and had become more favoured after the discovery of minerals there.[1] From these emigrants and from reports in the press some details of the situation in South Africa would have been known to the British public.

While Walter, as a very young man, was serving his apprenticeship as a painter and decorator (see Fig. 1, p. 6) and, when old enough, joining the local Company of the Lincolnshire Rifle Volunteers, tensions between the white settlers of Dutch and British origin were building up. After the occupation in 1806 of the Dutch Batavian Republic by the British and after the abolition of slavery in 1834, on which much of their prosperity depended, many Dutch settlers had joined the Great Trek and moved east and north by stages into the interior. Commonly known as the Boers, from the Dutch word for farmer, the Volk, as they called themselves, eventually crossed the Orange and Vaal rivers and established the two Boer Republics of the Orange Free State and the Transvaal. The Transvaal had been ratified by the British as an independent republic in 1852, followed by the Orange Free State in 1854.

The discovery of diamonds in the Orange Free State in 1870 led to the annexation of the town of Kimberley to Cape Colony in 1871 and, in 1877, to the

3

proclamation of the Transvaal as a British Crown Colony. In 1880, following the annexation, Paul Kruger led a Boer rebellion which became known as the First Anglo-Boer War. After the humiliating defeat of the British in February 1881 at the Battle of Majuba, a name which became a rallying cry for British soldiers in the Boer War, independence was restored to the Transvaal in 1884.[2]

The rush to the Witwatersrand in the Transvaal, when gold was discovered there in 1886, set up new tensions. Not only was there unrest among the *uit-landers*, as new arrivals were called, over their lack of political rights, but the commercial interests of gold magnates such as Cecil Rhodes, Barney Barnato,[3] Alfred Beit, and others, began to create pressure, largely undercover, for political control of the two Boer states.

The tension continued to build until, in 1895, with the covert support of Rhodes, Dr Storr Jameson, Rhodes's right-hand man in the new Chartered Company in Rhodesia, led a band of Company police and British uitlanders in an abortive attack on Johannesburg.[4] The Jameson Raid was mounted in the belief that the uitlanders would rise in support but this did not happen. After Jameson was defeated and captured at Doornkop, Kruger, with great diplomacy, had him deported to stand trial in London. Documents incriminating Rhodes in the affair were also captured and he was forced to resign as Prime Minister of the Cape. The Raid alerted the Boers to the lengths to which British interests would go to transfer the mineral wealth of the Orange Free State and the Transvaal to British control.

In 1897, in the wake of the Jameson Raid, Joseph Chamberlain, the Colonial Secretary, nominated Sir Alfred Milner as High Commissioner in South Africa with a brief to restore confidence in British rule.[5] However Milner, a staunch imperialist, believed that restoring good relations with the Republics was not enough. They must be returned to the imperial fold in the interests of a united Empire. With this in mind, Milner sought over the next two years to undermine the peace negotiations between the Boers and the Colonial Government. With the covert help of the gold magnates and the British uitlanders, Milner succeeded not only in aborting the Bloemfontein Conference of June 1899 but in persuading the British War Office to send troops to South Africa to reinforce the military garrison there. Milner represented to the British authorities that a strong military presence was the surest way of averting war.[6]

The failure of the Bloemfontein Conference and the imminent arrival of British troops in the territory alarmed Kruger, now President of the Transvaal, into hastening the organisation of the Volk into a citizen army of independent commandos armed with modern rifles and field guns. At the same time he continued to negotiate with the British but all Boer concessions on matters such as uitlander franchise were blocked by Milner's counter-demands.[7] Kruger was forced to the conclusion that British intentions were no less than the annexation of the Orange Free State and the Transvaal.[8] Consequently, on 9 October 1899, an ultimatum was delivered to the British Agent in the Transvaal demanding withdrawal of all British troops from the borders of the Republics and, indeed, from the whole of South Africa. When the specified forty-eight hours had elapsed with no reply from the British, a state of war was declared on 11 October.[9]

Walter Barley could not have foreseen when war was declared that he would be called on to play a part in it. It was confidently expected that British military might would triumph before Christmas; but, after a series of defeats in December 1899, active service units were raised early in 1900 from a variety of volunteer bodies and dispatched to South Africa. Walter Barley was one of those who embarked on the greatest adventure of their lives.

Men, such as Walter, at the bottom of the military hierarchy were rarely in a position to follow the strategies and sequence of events of the war, much less to influence them. In order to place in perspective the experiences of Walter and his comrades as the war progressed, a summary of the main events is offered at the end of each series of documents.

BACKGROUND TO LETTERS OF THE BOER WAR

One of the least well-known aspects of the South African War of 1899–1902, alternatively known as the Second Anglo-Boer War and popularly as the Boer War, is the recruitment for active service, and the war experiences in South Africa, of the Volunteers. Renamed the Territorial Army in 1909, these part-time soldiers were members of the Volunteer Battalions attached to Regular Army regiments. After the 'Black Week' of 10–15 December 1899, when the British Army suffered humiliating defeats with heavy losses at the hands of the Boers – at Stormberg, Magersfontein and Colenso – the strength of the British Army in South Africa was dangerously depleted. Appeals were made in Britain, and indeed in many other parts of the British Empire, for men to offer themselves for active service. The Volunteers were limited by their regulations to home service but a change in these made it possible for them to volunteer. From 'playing at war' the chosen ones were pitchforked into the battle line. My great-uncle, Walter Shearsmith Barley from Scunthorpe in the County of Lincoln, was one of these.

Against the major political and military events of the war, the letters of a private soldier may seem unimportant. Such letters, however, in addition to their intrinsic human interest, are important for an understanding of how the momentous events of those years appeared to ordinary citizens in Britain. Their only sources of information were small provincial newspapers and letters from the men serving in South Africa.

Fig. 1 Walter Barley, *c.* 1890, as a journeyman painter and decorator, holding the tools of his trade.

The letters of the Boer War present a landmark in the history of communication. Those from private soldiers to relatives and friends at home were the first wartime letters to be written by a newly literate lower class, following the education reforms of 1870 and 1880. This was particularly true of the Volunteers since they were, in general, recruited from the upper working or lower middle classes. Most were tradesmen, shopworkers and clerks who would have received a basic elementary education and left school around the age of twelve years, as they were entitled to do if they could show proficiency in basic literacy. Some may have chosen to stay at school longer, but it was not until 1902, long after Walter's schooldays were over, that schooling was made compulsory between the ages of five and fourteen and fees were abolished for the elementary level.

A second factor that makes the letters accessible to later generations is that this was the last major war in which there was little or no censorship. Walter's letters bear no disfiguring black lines, even when he openly criticised the system and his officers. He was able to tell his family back home exactly where he was, what he was doing and how he felt.

At the time Walter left school in the 1880s, almost all boys of his class would have gone on to serve apprenticeships in various trades. They were articled to a master craftsman for the seven years customary in the practice inherited from the medieval guild system. At the end of the seven years, if deemed satisfactory, apprentices became journeymen who could then offer their services freely or take up work in their own right. Walter was articled to a painter and decorator and an existing photograph shows him, holding the tools of his trade, when he became a journeyman (Fig. 1).

It is difficult for us, in this age of widely available travel and the revolution in communications, to appreciate what a change from small-town life it must have been for those part-time soldiers to travel overseas to the zone of war. There is no evidence that Walter had ever been more than fifty or sixty miles from home – to Lincoln, the headquarters of his battalion; to Sheffield, to visit his sister and family; to Cleethorpes, probably, for a Bank Holiday outing; and to wherever the annual camp for the Volunteers was held. These were his horizons. His knowledge of the world, as we see from his letters, was gleaned mainly from local newspapers and popular magazines. He mentions books in one letter but of what kind is not clear.

To have a son travel so far away, and for what at the time was deemed to be such a worthy cause, was of the utmost importance and pride. Walter's family was no exception. His letters, carefully preserved and, fortunately for legibility nearly a hundred years later, written in indelible pencil, were found in the back of a cupboard in the family home when the last of his nieces to remain unmarried, died in the early 1980s. With them, carefully clipped from newspapers or journals but often, unfortunately for the researcher, without acknowledgement of source or exact date, were items of news, articles and poems. Also lovingly preserved were photographs of Walter and his Volunteer comrades, taken both in England and in South Africa. These letters and memorabilia open up to us the world of one man at a dramatic point in his country's history.

The aim of this work is not to follow in detail the events of the war as they unfolded, although the brief summary offered at the end of each chapter places the experiences of the Lincolnshire Volunteers in perspective. It is, in the first place, to offer a picture, seen through the eyes of one man, his comrades and his family, of what the men experienced from the time of their recruitment and send-off to their triumphant return home at the end of their term of service. To Walter's letters have been added those of several of his comrades, and even additional ones from Walter himself, as they were printed in local papers. Secondly, the documents present a compelling, often harrowing, picture of the conditions endured and the experiences encountered by the private soldiers at the bottom of the military hierarchy. Walter's comments on the way he and his companions were treated by the War Office, and, nearer at hand, by their own officers, present an illuminating picture. We learn of the erratic and niggardly distribution of pay, to the extent that privates on 1s 3d a day were expected to finance the repair of their own boots and the purchase of any food in excess of the meagre army rations. We hear of the often ragged state of uniforms, and of boots in such poor condition that some of the soldiers, including Walter himself on at least one occasion, were unable to march into battle. Most poignantly of all, we hear of the disease and death surrounding them throughout the campaign which robbed them of comrades, often without a bullet being fired.[10]

A third strand revealed by the documents is the attitudes of the ordinary citizen of small-town Britain to the causes and events of the Boer War. Items of news from local papers fill out the picture of the war as the people of Walter's home town would have understood it. Walter, as well as describing his day-to-day life and the military events in which he was engaged, also shows a lively appreciation of the climate, scenery, wildlife and flora of the country he found himself in.

THE BARLEY LETTERS

As Walter was unmarried, the letters were written to his mother and sisters. Their letters, written to him in South Africa, have not survived so we are only able to deduce what they wrote from the answers he gave them.

It is noticeable that the letters concentrate more on family and home news than on events of the war, other than those in which Walter was closely involved.

It is interesting to speculate whether the tone of his letters would have been different and focused more on the strategy of the war had he not been writing to women – his mother and the 'giddy girls', as he called his sisters.

An interesting feature of Walter's letters is the way in which they improve in calligraphy, syntax, spelling and expression over the period of writing. The early letters are written in a large hand, with many spelling mistakes and rudimentary punctuation. They give the impression of a man who, since leaving school, had little need to write more than the estimates and bills required by his trade. The later letters improve both in syntax and in power of expression, some being long, well-phrased and showing an ability to convey both feelings and observation.

A reason for the improvement in Walter's writing ability may lie not only in practice but also in the fact that he was in close contact with men better educated than himself. From Walter's remark in an early letter that he had written home for both Charlesworth and Skinner, it is clear that the men helped one another and, no doubt, the better educated helped him when he needed it.

Walter uses Lincolnshire dialect throughout the letters but it is less noticeable in the later ones. In the early letters, for example, he regularly uses 'while' for until, and 'against' or 'again' for close to. Later he mainly used the latter words. Walter also used some dialect terms no longer in use such as 'pissmires' and 'bug-blinding', explanations for which are to be found in the Glossary.

WALTER BARLEY AND HIS FAMILY

Walter Shearsmith Barley was born on 30 April 1870 at Brigg in the County of Lincoln, the second child and only son of John and Eliza Barley, née Eliza Williams Knott. His second name, Shearsmith, came from his maternal grandmother, Mary Shearsmith, who married Henry Knott of Louth about 1830. Henry Knott was a boat owner who plied his trade on the rivers and canals between north Lincolnshire and the Staffordshire Potteries. His main cargo was pottery but no details of his boat have survived. In view of the width of the canals around the Etruria factories, it would have been a narrowboat.

According to family tradition Henry Knott's wife and children did not accompany him, as did many families in the latter half of the nineteenth century, but lived in Brigg so that the children could attend school. Recorded on a page in my possession, torn from a family bible, are the names of six children born to the family, of whom three, or possibly four, died in early childhood. Only two reached adulthood – Eliza and a much younger brother, George. My aunts Lenna and Ada, the nieces of Walter Barley, had in their possession two Staffordshire pottery money boxes, with the names of Eliza Knott and George Knott painted on them. George's was broken but Eliza's came to me when the aunts died. Henry Knott is said to have brought them back for the children from one of his trips to the Potteries.

Eliza Williams Knott, born 5 September 1836, married John Barley, on 19 May 1863. On the marriage certificate John is listed as a labourer but later in life he was a drayman for a local brewery. Three children were born, the eldest, Lillia (Lillie), on 31 March 1864, followed by Walter in 1870 and a second daughter, Kate, on 10 December 1871. John Barley died at Brigg in September 1895 at the age of 55 years. By this time Lillie had married Charles James Stubbins, a master bricklayer of Brigg, on 12 June 1889 and started the family of girls, Walter's nieces. A first child, a boy, had been stillborn. He was followed, in November 1892, by Dorothy, who died at the age of six years from complications of measles. Four more girls arrived in quick succession – Lenna, 18 April 1894; Ada, 30 July 1895; May, 17 May 1897; and Marian, my mother, always known as Molly, on 17 October 1899.

At some time between the death of John Barley and 1899, Walter and his mother moved from Brigg to Scunthorpe, then only a small town close to Frodingham, Crosby, Brumby and Ashby. It is probable that there was more demand for Walter's skills as a painter and decorator as Scunthorpe and Frodingham were growing steel towns.[11] A three-storey terrace house was rented at 29 Winterton Road, where Walter set up his business. Next door was a family named Threadgould and Kate married one of the sons, Harry Threadgould.

At the time of Walter's departure for South Africa, his sister Lillie and her family were living in Sheffield. Charles Stubbins had moved there from Brigg to seek work, but in 1901, not long after Walter's return, he brought his family to Scunthorpe and moved in with his wife's mother. Charles found work in the steel-works as a 'fettler', the bricklayer who performed the specialist task of replacing the brick linings of the furnaces.[12] He worked there for the rest of his life, and died at work while working inside a furnace. His widow sought Workmen's Compensation, claiming that he had been overcome by fumes in the furnace, but the firm denied responsibility by claiming that he had had a heart attack before being gassed. No compensation was ever paid.

Kate and Harry Threadgould lived at Misterton Soss, four miles south of Gainsborough, where Harry was in charge of one of the pumping stations on the River Trent. They had no children so Kate played a large part in the upbringing of her sister's family. Each in turn spent many months at Misterton. Ada was tubercular from an early age and, when not away in a sanatorium, was nursed by her aunt at Misterton. The two youngest, May and Molly, both remembered being put on Skelton the carrier's cart early in the morning, well wrapped up for the slow journey to Gainsborough. There they were met by Auntie Kate in a horse and trap.

Molly began these journeys when she was less than three years old. She remembered being roused and dressed before first light and placed, still half-asleep, in the carrier's cart. Kate and Harry Threadgould left Misterton in 1931 and lived for the rest of their lives at Hemswell, near Lincoln. Kate died there in 1940, shortly after her husband.

Of the four Stubbins sisters, Lenna and Ada never married but stayed at home with their widowed mother. Grandma Barley died on 29 January 1922. Shortly after her husband's death in 1923, Lillie and her daughters moved from Winterton Road to a smaller house in Mary Street, nearer the centre of the town. Ada, being regarded as delicate, never worked. She was an accomplished pianist who, throughout her life, offered her services to many organisations as an accompanist. Lenna learned her trade as a dressmaker and tailoress and much of her working life was spent in the alterations department of Bee's shop in Scunthorpe. She provided the only regular income. Lenna also considered herself to be delicate as she had had an operation for appendicitis in her twenties. From that time until her death over fifty years later, she wore a dressing over her 'wound', and insisted on having a milk pudding every day to line her stomach before the main meal, prepared for her return from work by her mother and sister. Lillia Stubbins died in 1945. After Lenna's retirement, the two sisters moved to an old people's bungalow in Ashby and lived there until their deaths. Lenna died in April 1970 at the age of 76, and Ada, despite her poor health, lived to the grand old age of 88 years, dying in 1983.

May, 'Baby' of the letters, asserted her independence at an early age by looking for work in Kingston upon Hull, always known as Hull. She worked as a clerk in various offices and there met George Sergeant, an accounts clerk. They were married at Scunthorpe Church on her birthday, 17 May 1922. May's life was a tragic one which she bore with characteristic courage. Not only had she lost her beloved Uncle Walter when he died in 1910, but her three children – Geoffrey was born in 1923, Kathleen in 1925 and Shirley in 1930 – all died young. Kathleen died of pneumonia at the age of ten months. Shirley was always delicate and at the age of five, just as she was about to start school, she caught measles, was taken into hospital where she added chickenpox to her ills, and died of heart failure after being sent home as incurable. Geoffrey lived, married and had two children, but died of cancer at the age of forty. George, May's husband, died of heart disease in 1952. May lived on, comforted by her two grandchildren, until she died at the age of 92 in 1990. I was always very close to her and it is from her that many of the memories of Walter have come.

My mother, Molly, was only an infant when Walter went to South Africa and less than two years old when he returned. She seems to have been a somewhat unwelcome addition to the family, possibly because, after a string of girls, she was not the hoped-for boy. Walter, in one of his letters, promised Lenna that when he got back he would 'turn that baby out'. Molly was always very sensitive about her position in the family and, although I shared and discussed the letters with May, I never dared to introduce the topic to Molly. In addition to wishing to turn her out, Walter had not brought her a Kruger penny from South Africa as he had for the others, and she never quite forgot that. He did, however, bring coral necklaces for the two youngest girls, which are now in the possession of my two daughters.

Molly was the only one of the family to gain a higher education, training as a teacher at Sheffield Training College. She taught for only two years before marrying Walter Bone of Doncaster, who, by that time, had moved to Scunthorpe and set up as an estate agent. Lenna and Ada never quite forgave him for marrying Molly and taking away the income from her teaching they had counted upon. They regarded her as their investment as they claimed to have been denied the wages she could have been earning instead of studying. In fact, after the death of her father, the family was too poor to pay for her training and she borrowed the money from a generous elderly friend. Walter Bone repaid the debt when they married.

In 1930, when my brother, Brian, was six, my sister, Margaret, nearly two and I was three years old, my family, following in Walter Barley's footsteps, emigrated to South Africa. The family returned to England in 1936.

OTHER PEOPLE MENTIONED IN THE LETTERS

Many of the people named in the letters cannot be traced. Two people named most frequently can, however, be identified.

John Fowler was a member of the Volunteers, holding the rank of Colour Sergeant. He was a draper who worked in the drapery department of the local Co-operative Society. May remembered him as a staunch friend throughout her childhood. She told me of the disappointment of the Stubbins children when chickenpox prevented them from going on an annual outing to Cleethorpes. John Fowler, who organised the trip, sought to comfort the little girls by bringing them each a present – a doll each for three of them but May, the tomboy of the family, was brought a ball.

George Jubb – George or Jubby in the letters – was a lodger at 29 Winterton Road during his bachelor days. He moved out when he married Carrie but lived close enough to help out with the 'garden' during Walter's absence. This garden, so beloved of Walter, was an allotment as the Winterton Road house had only a back yard.

Chapter 2

Background to Recruitment

THE VOLUNTEER MOVEMENT

The Volunteers and their successors, the Territorial Army, have been part-time civilian battalions attached to regiments of the Regular Army from their inception. The first Volunteer units were raised in 1859 at the time of fears of a French invasion. The reasons of the British Government for this move are somewhat obscure and it can only be assumed that it resulted from an over-reaction to the situation in Europe, possibly on the part of the Prime Minister, Lord Palmerston. Napoleon III of France was, at the time, engaged in trying to maximise his influence in Italy by confronting the considerable power of the Austrians in the northern states of that country. Opinion in Britain was divided but Palmerston, in opposition to Queen Victoria, took the side of Italian patriots whose aim was the unification of Italy.[13] Why it should have been believed that Napoleon posed an invasion threat to Britain when his attention and efforts were engaged elsewhere is not clear, but the outcome was the setting up of a volunteer force which could, if necessary, be mobilised to defend the nation's shores.

The role of the newly formed body was made explicit in a circular sent, in 1859, to all Lords-Lieutenant and was enshrined in the oath taken by all who joined. Each volunteer was committed to serve 'Her Majesty in Great Britain for the defence of the same against all her enemies', but service was limited to situations of 'actual invasion or appearance of an enemy in force on the coast'. The Volunteer movement was, therefore, limited to home service.[14]

From 1859 to the recruitment crisis at the outbreak of the South African War in 1899, the restriction on overseas service had held good. The only occasion on which representation was made for Volunteers to be deployed overseas was in 1882 when a mounted infantry corps from the Volunteers was requested to help subdue an insurrection against the British in Egypt. The request was refused but a

13

small precedent was created when a detachment of the Post Office Battalion – the 24th Middlesex Rifle Volunteers – was sent to administer postal services.[15] In 1894–95 a select committee considered the role of the Volunteers but its terms of reference only covered crisis situations within the United Kingdom and the possibility of service overseas was not discussed.[16]

Fig. 2 K Company (Frodingham) of the Lincolnshire Rifle Volunteers, Lincolnshire Regiment, in ceremonial uniform. Back row, from left: G.A. Robshaw, A. Charlesworth, W.F. Marris, J.W. Drury. Middle row: T. Hockney, T.G. Beech, W.S. Barley, F.A. Skinner. Front row: T. Rhodes, C.M. Skinner.

ACTIVITIES OF THE VOLUNTEERS

The organisation of the Volunteers into battalions attached to Regular Army regiments developed over the years from 1859. The number of such battalions depended on the numbers of men wishing to join. If a battalion became over-manned, it was divided into two based on geographic locations. Each battalion was broken up into companies, again geographically, so that the group to which a Volunteer owed his first allegiance was local and of manageable size. It was in these companies that the Volunteers held their training sessions and formed the strong relationships that, in the Boer War, carried them through the dangers and privations. Walter Barley belonged to K Company (Frodingham), 1st Battalion (Lincoln) of the Lincolnshire Rifle Volunteers, Lincolnshire Regiment (Fig. 2).[17]

In keeping with their part-time status, the companies of the Volunteer movement met, usually in their own drill halls, to practice the skills of warfare. Rifle practice took up much of their time but drill, to the extent practised in the Regular Army, did not play such an important role except, perhaps, at the annual camps. Public occasions and church parades would have seen the Volunteers, in full ceremonial uniform, marching behind their bands. Much of the rest of their time together was taken up with what could better be described as club, rather than military, activities. Because of their part-time and volunteer status, the movement was often sarcastically described as 'playing at soldiers'.

The occasions on which the military skills of the Volunteers had been called upon were extremely rare, amounting to no more than occasional minor civil disturbances, so that the movement had no experience of strategy or execution in a wartime situation. Until the outbreak of the Boer War and the call to arms in South Africa, the part-time soldiers had enjoyed activities more akin to boy scouting than to soldiering.[18]

Unlike the Regular Army, which recruited its private soldiers largely from the lowest ranks of British society, most of whom were illiterate, the Volunteers were drawn mainly from the artisan classes which in present-day terms would be described as lower-middle-class. Shopworkers, clerks and skilled artisans made up the majority of the membership of the Volunteer battalions.[19] Almost all the men who joined the movement would have come from families that had taken advantage of the elementary education reforms from 1870. They were, therefore, the first generation of serving soldiers who could write home of their experiences. Hence, the volume of written information contained in the letters of soldiers serving in South Africa exceeds that from previous campaigns.[20]

CRISIS IN SOUTH AFRICA

On 11 October 1899, following the expiry of the ultimatum to the British by President Kruger of the Transvaal, the Boers declared war. The situation, as it was very soon to affect the Volunteer movement, was that the Regular Army was seriously undermanned and the War Office neither adequately equipped to supply the numbers that would soon be enlisted nor expecting serious resistance from the Boer South African Republics.[21] Never had the cry, 'It will be over by Christmas', been more widely and confidently used. Neither the Government nor the people of Britain believed that a small nation of farmers in a far-flung corner of the great British Empire could stand against the might of British arms. They were soon to learn differently. The Boer commandos on their fleet horses were expert marksmen who could use the terrain they knew so well to attack without warning and disappear again. In the early encounters between the two sides the British army, whose military organisation and tactics had changed little since the Napoleonic wars, could not respond effectively. However much the army railed against a 'cowardly' enemy that would not stand and fight, they had little answer to these guerrilla tactics. So it was that early battle honours went to the Boers.

The events that brought home to the British public the seriousness of the situation in South Africa were the defeats in what came to be called 'Black Week'. Between the 10th and the 15th of December 1899, the British forces suffered three major defeats – at Stormberg, Magersfontein and Colenso. Not only were the troops decisively defeated with high casualties, but 2,000 men were taken prisoner and moved to Pretoria. In addition to this series of disasters, the towns of Kimberley, Mafeking and Ladysmith were attacked and beseiged. The development of the telegraph, first used in the Crimean War of 1854 to 1856, ensured that both government and people received the news almost as it occurred. The shock of the realisation that the British Army was not invincible, and the long lists of casualties, led to an upsurge of emotion and jingoistic patriotism. Many rushed to enlist. Among these were the Volunteers, some of whom were Reservists who were immediately called to the colours. The rest clamoured for the terms of their service to be changed so that they, too, could serve in South Africa.[22]

UNITS IN THE DEFENCE OF THE REALM

To understand the manner in which enlistment for South Africa took place in the chaotic first few months of the war, it is necessary to distinguish between the different units that made up the defence forces of the United Kingdom.[23]

In the first place was the **Regular Army**, which, since the Crimean War, had been kept at very low strength. The second half of the nineteenth century had seen no large-scale war and the army had been used mainly for garrisoning the British colonies and engaging in small colonial wars. In fact, there was never a year when the army was not engaged somewhere in the colonial territories.[24] At the time of the outbreak of the Boer War there were 20,000 men in South Africa, about half of whom had been withdrawn from India at the beginning of the crisis. Recruitment to the Regular Army was immediately put in hand but the demands from South Africa after 'Black Week' were for the urgent despatch of 50,000 men.[25] However, the processing, equipping and training of new recruits took time.

The next to be called upon were the **Reservists**. These were former Regular soldiers, members of the Militia or Volunteers who had signed on for military duty if called. Walter's friend Arthur Lockwood, 'Lockey', was one of these, but whether he was an ex-soldier or a Volunteer who had signed for duty is not clear. The Reservists were mobilised in the early weeks of the war and despatched to South Africa. Some were foot soldiers and some mounted infantry which came to be known as the 'MI'. They were, in general, inadequately trained for the task in hand.

The **Militia** had its roots far back in history. Its members were obliged to report for duty if called but their role, unless they were Reservists, was the defence of the homeland and they could not be deployed overseas. They played no active part in the Boer War but were used to fill gaps in home defence in the absence of the Regular Army overseas.

The next unit to be formed was the **Imperial Yeomanry**. It was noted in the first weeks of the war that the success of the Boers rested on their mobility on horseback. A mounted force was, therefore, felt to be necessary and the War Office was immediately besieged by members of the aristocracy and others who wished to set up mounted units at their own expense. Out of this came some of the most colourful units to serve at the Cape. Many took their names from those who raised and financed them, hence Lovat's Horse, Paget's Horse, and so on. It was soon found, however, that although such units gave good service, mobility alone was not enough. Knowledge of the terrain, which the Boers had in abundance, and the ability of the horses to withstand both the poor fodder of the veld and the endemic horse sickness caused by the tsetse fly, to which the tough Boer ponies had some immunity, were also vital. The units of the Imperial Yeomanry, many made up of the tenants and retainers of landowners as well as gentlemen foxhunters and sportsmen, were untrained but compensated in some measure for their lack of military discipline by the enthusiasm they brought to the task.

A unit which combined elements of both the Yeomanry and the Volunteers was the **City Imperial Volunteers**. Raised and financed largely by the City of London, it mustered almost a thousand men drawn not only from the Volunteer battalions of London and the surrounding counties but also by direct recruitment. It was the best known of the volunteer units to serve in South Africa as both mounted and infantry detachments.[26] The CIV received so much attention and praise that they were thoroughly resented by many in other units whose names were not as regularly paraded before the public. Walter complained about them when news came of their demobilisation while he and his companions waited impatiently for news of their own return to Britain.

Finally it was to the **Volunteers** that attention turned. They had qualities that some of the other auxiliary units lacked in that they were disciplined and trained. The terms of their charter which limited them to home service were a major stumbling-block. For some weeks the argument raged at the War Office, as the top echelons of the Regular Army and those with influence in the Volunteer battalions fought it out.[27] Eventually, in December, the War Office made its decision and a circular, under the signature of Lord Wolseley, Commander-in-Chief, was sent out.[28] This document stated the rules under which auxiliaries such as the Volunteers could be called for duty in South Africa. Active service companies were to be drawn from each of the Volunteer battalions. The number and composition of each company were specified, the skills and qualifications of each man laid down and the arrangements for selection, equipment and transport to South Africa delineated. A significant condition of service was that the men were to volunteer for one year only but, although it was clear that the contracts were short-term, it was never spelt out when the term would begin or end. The letters of Walter Barley and other documents of the day illustrate the confusion and unrest that this lack of precision caused in the ranks of those serving overseas.

Although the conditions of service for the Volunteers had been specified, the legal limitation which restricted them to service within the United Kingdom had not been clarified. The passing of the Imminent National Danger Act in 1900 regularised the position, but not without opposition from some politicians who argued that it would completely change the purpose of the movement. Many felt that the Act contained a hint of conscription, to which they were strongly opposed.[29] Despite these objections the Act became law, and arrangements for forming the Imperial Yeomanry, active service companies of the Volunteers and the City Imperial Volunteers, and dispatching them to South Africa, proceeded apace.

Fig. 3 Walter (second from the left in the back row) in football kit with the Volunteers team, 1890s.

THE LINCOLNSHIRE RIFLE VOLUNTEERS

The Lincolnshire Rifle Volunteers was one of the earliest Volunteer battalions to be set up, being inaugurated at Lincoln on 26 October 1859. By the 1880s two battalions had been commissioned, the 1st Volunteer Battalion at Lincoln and the 2nd at Grantham. These titles were approved in 1883. In June 1900 the 1st Battalion was deemed to be too large and was reorganised into two battalions, thus forming the 3rd Battalion at Grimsby. Within these battalions were companies located at different places within the region. K Company of the 1st Volunteer Battalion (Lincoln), to which Walter belonged, was located at Frodingham.[30]

It is likely that Walter Barley joined the Volunteers in Brigg before moving to Scunthorpe, as a company was formed there in 1891, the year in which he reached the age of 21. The Volunteers played an important role in Walter's life. He was an enthusiastic member, joining in all their activities and making many friends among the men. A photograph found with the letters shows him posing in full kit with his company's football team (Fig. 3). His proficiency with a rifle enabled him not only to be chosen for active service in South Africa but, as he reports in one letter, to win prizes at the annual Tradesmen's Prize Shoot. The highlight of his year was the annual camp for all the Lincoln contingents and he much regretted missing it when away in South Africa.

Another of the photographs found with Walter's letters is of the Lincolnshire Rifle Volunteers at Lincoln in 1900, commissioned and reproduced by the *Lincoln Leader*. The long caption beneath the picture, which is quoted below, illustrates the method of selection and the process through which Volunteers around the country went before embarking for South Africa.

THE LINCOLNSHIRE INFANTRY VOLUNTEERS
FOR SOUTH AFRICA, FEBRUARY, 1900
Captain H.E. Newsum (Lincoln); Lieutenant H. Stephenson
(Barton-on-Humber); Lieutenant R.F. Lee (Grantham)

The call for British Volunteers to join the forces engaged in the war against the Boer South African Republics was published on December 16th 1899. Lincolnshire was one of the earliest counties to respond. The War Office required from this county one Company of Infantry selected from the two territorial Volunteers Battalions, and numbering altogether 116, viz.: 113 non-commissioned officers and men and three officers. Very many more than were required eagerly proffered their services, and the selections were accordingly made, after due

The Lincolnshire Infantry Volunteers for South Africa, February, 1900.
Captain H. E. Newsum (Lincoln): Lieutenant H Stephenson (Barton-on-Humber): Lieutenant R. F. Lee (Grantham).

Fig. 4 The Lincolnshire Rifle Volunteers at Lincoln in February 1900 before departure for South Africa. (By kind permission of the Museum of Lincolnshire Life, Lincoln.)

examination, by the Colonel of the 1st Battalion (Colonel J.G.Williams who first joined the Volunteer Force 41 years ago), and the Colonel of the 2nd Battalion (Colonel James Hutchinson). From among the officers, the Colonel Commanding the Tenth Regimental District (Col. Verner C.B.) selected Captain H.E. Newsum of Lincoln (seen standing in the left centre of the above photograph), Captain R.F. Lee of Grantham (standing to the rear of the Company), and Captain H.Stephenson of Barton-on-Humber (at the right angle). In the Active Service Company, Captains Lee and Stephenson sink their rank and serve as Lieutenants under Captain Newsum. The men assembled at Grantham for musketry practice on January 25th 1900, and the townspeople of Grantham entertained them in a very hearty fashion. After spending four days there they arrived in Lincoln on January 30th. On Wednesday, January 31st, they attended a service in the Cathedral, when a sermon was preached by the Lord Bishop (Dr.

King) in a great congregation. The next night the Volunteers were banquetted in the Lincoln Drill Hall. From all parts of Lincolnshire gifts of necessary articles were received, and the Mayor of Lincoln (Col. J.G.Williams) opened a 'send-off' fund. The above photograph [Fig. 4] was taken on the South Common, Lincoln, a few days before the Company left for South Africa. The departure took place on the 17th February, from Southampton on the Guelph.

Walter's company was listed among those of the 1st Battalion Detachment.

K COMPANY (FRODINGHAM).
 Private W.S. Barley
   " *A. Charlesworth*
   " *J.W. Drury*
   " *T. Hockney*
   " *W.T. Marris*
   " *T. Rhodes*
   " *F. Skinner*

Notes to Part One

1. C. Swaisland, *Servants and Gentlewomen to the Golden Land: The Emigration of Single Women from Britain to Southern Africa 1820–1939*, Oxford and Pietermaritzburg, 1993, Chapter 3.
2. A useful introduction to the situation in South Africa up to the outbreak of the South African War may be found in T.R.H. Davenport, *South Africa: A Modern History*, London, 1977, Part 1.
3. The story of the rise to fame and wealth of Rhodes and Barnato is told in J. Leasor, *Rhodes and Barnato: The Premier and the Prancer*, London, 1997.
4. For an account of the Jameson Raid and its significance see T. Pakenham, *The Boer War*, London, 1979, Prologue.
5. Ibid., p. 22.
6. Ibid., Chapter 6, especially p. 69 – Milner assures the British Cabinet that a strong military presence in South Africa would mean that there would be no war.
7. J. Meintjes, *President Paul Kruger*, London, 1974, pp. 225–6.
8. Ibid., p. 227.
9. Ibid., pp. 230–1.
10. See Part Three of this work for detailed accounts of these conditions.
11. For a history of the development of the steel industry in Lincolnshire see R. Creed and A. Coult, *Steeltown: The Story of the Men and Women Who Built an Industry*, 1990, Beverley, E. Yorkshire, Chapter 1.
12. Ibid., Appendix 1, p. 146, 'Glossary of Iron and Steelmaking Terms'.
13. For a discussion of the Italian Question of 1859 which led to the establishment of the Volunteer Movement see G.M. Trevelyan, *History of England*, 3rd Edition, London, 1945, p. 654.
14. R. Price, *An Imperial War and the British Working Class*, London, 1972, Chapter 5.
15. Ibid., p. 184.
16. Ibid., pp.184–5.
17. K.W.S. Goodson, 'Notes on the Genealogy of the Volunteer Force & Territorial Army', MS in the Museum of Lincolnshire Life, Lincoln, p. 3.
18. G. Cousins, *The Defenders: A History of the British Volunteer*, London, 1968, p. 141.
19. Price – on the class structure of the Volunteer Movement, pp. 216–19.
20. Ibid. – on the educational standards of the Volunteers, 1896–1902, p. 198.

21. Cousins, pp. 127–30.
22. Price, p. 182.
23. Ibid., pp. 180–1.
24. For a discussion of colonial wars see B. Farwell, *Queen Victoria's Little Wars*, London, 1973.
25. Cousins, p. 127.
26. Price – on the City Imperial Volunteers, p. 191.
27. Ibid. – on the arguments and negotiations in the British Parliament before Army Order No. 1 became law, pp. 183–9.
28. See Appendix 1: Army Order No. 1, 1900 – Rules for the Employment of Auxiliaries.
29. Price, p. 188.
30. Goodson, 'Notes'.

PART TWO

The Letters and Supporting Documents

Chapter 3

Departure and Voyage

December 1899 to March 1900

> *Duke's Son – cook's son – son of a hundred kings –*
>   *(Fifty thousand horse and foot going to Table Bay!)*
> *Each of 'em doing his country's work*
>   *(and who's to look after their things?)*
> *Pass the hat for your credit's sake, and pay – pay – pay!*

Kipling – 'The Absent-minded Beggar'[1]

Lindsey and Lincolnshire Star, 27 January 1900, p. 5

VOLUNTEERS LEAVE FOR ACTIVE SERVICE

The Scunthorpe Volunteers, Lance Corp. Beech, Privates W.S. Barley, J.W. Drury, F. Skinner, T. Hockney, T. Rhodes, Alec Charlesworth and W.T. Marris were entertained to dinner at the Blue Bell Hotel. With the exception of Charlesworth, all the Volunteers were bachelors.

On Thursday, 25 January, they formed up in full kit at the Drill Hall and, led by the Volunteer Band, marched to the railway station.

The platform and the railway bridge were filled with people and we venture to say that there never had been such a sight in Scunthorpe before. Many affecting scenes were witnessed at the station at the last moment between the men and their relatives and friends.

Fog signals were placed on the line as the train left. Later news

*was received from Lincoln that all had passed and gone on to
Grantham to join the 2nd Battalion, Lincolnshire Regiment.*

*The men were all in high spirits and one of them swears he will
go for Old Kruger's whiskers if only he gets a chance.*

The reference to 'having passed' relates to the medical and rifle efficiency tests
required for all those joining the active service companies. It is obvious from a
later letter that it was Walter Marris who promised 'to go for old Kruger's
whiskers'.

Letter 1

Friday Night
Granby Inn

Dear Ma

Just a line or two to let you know we arrived safely and passed,
then at night came to Grantham and are billited out at public houses.
We expect coming to Lincoln again middle of next week and having a
day or two furlough. We are going on a sixteen mile march tomorrow,
that's bad. We have been shooting today it was cold, they are giving us
some stiff drills. We have got all our Kharki suits. Well I think that is
all for the present. I will write again so goodbye for the present.

With best love
Walter

(Written from the Granby Inn, Market Place, Grantham.)

Lindsey and Lincolnshire Star, 27 January 1900, p. 5

THE LINCOLNSHIRE VOLUNTEERS OFF TO THE FRONT

*Two battalions of Lincolnshire Volunteers – 100 men under Captain
Newsum, – left Grantham on Monday. There was a special service in
the Parish Church. At the Guildhall Lord Brownlow, the Lord
Lieutenant of the County, entertained the men to lunch and reviewed
them on St. Peter's Hill.*

*Lord Brownlow said that the men had taken upon themselves a
noble trust and a great responsibility, for they had undertaken to*

support the credit and honour not only of their county but of the country and the honour of their Queen. He reminded them that they had undertaken the credit and honour of the whole volunteer service. They, drawn from a higher class than the rest of the army, should show an example of discipline and good conduct and should show that the Volunteers were composed of God-fearing and honourable men.

Letter 2

Marquis of Granby
Lincoln

Jan 31/00

Dear Ma

We have left Grantham. We left last night and are at Lincoln now. I never received a letter there according to what Jhonny Fowler said so if you write do so before Friday has we leave then for Aldershot.

Me and Alec Charlesworth are invilids through the march on Saturday. We have all the skin of our heels and are being doctered, I also have influensa. I am as deaf as a stone. I can't hear the orders they give so I am off duty. We shall not get any leave the Captain said, before we sail so we can't come home. I should have liked to.

We went to Belton Park on Sunday afternoon, had tea in the Ball Room. Lady Brownlow shook hands with us all, and cried a bit then presented us with a wallet, a beauty too. On Monday night we were entertained to dinner by the Grantham tradespeople, the best I have ever sat down to. I will finish now has I am mixed up with the Influenza. Remember me to all. I will write again when we get to Aldershot so if you write to Lincoln write by return or I shan't get it.

Adress Private W S Barley
Marquis of Granby
Lincoln

With love, W

Letter 3 (Fig. 5)

Feb 6/1900
Marquis of Granby
Lincoln

Dear Ma

Another few lines to let you know I am about better but it as left me a bit deaf. I have had my ears syringed out at the docters, how are things going on. I dont think we shall get home at all now. We dont know when we sail. I dont care how soon as we shall miss all the fun and the Victoria Cross. I expect Kruger will give in when he sees our company, we have been attacking the boers this morning on Spion Kop, I killed seven.

We went yesterday afternoon to Branston Hall for a eight mile walk to tea. We were presented with 1 pair of socks, 2 hankerchiefs and one testiment, we ought to be good with the bibles we have. We have too many clothes now, two pairs of boots, they cost 25/- a pair, brown ones, and one pair of shoes.

I started work yesterday. My word they do give us socks, it is worse than work, we shall soon be has hard as nails. My knee has stood it champion. I hear Tom Beech is coming home, got the sack for being ill, poor fellow I am sorry for him, he has lost his voice.

Remember me to J Fowler, tell him I will drop him a line if I have time. I am writing four now. I have to write for Skinner & Charlesworth. I think that is all at present. Is Kate with you yet. With best love to you, and all.

Walter

This address will find me anywhere.

> Pte W S Barley
> No 3406
> Active Service Co
> 1st Vol Batt Line Regt
> Drill Hall, Lincoln

After the period of training, referred to by Walter as 'attacking the boers … on Spion Kop', the Volunteers left Lincoln for Southampton and embarked on the *Guelph* on 17 February. They followed in the wake of the Regular Army detachment of the Lincolnshire Regiment which had left for South Africa on 4 January and landed in Cape Town on the 27th. After a few days there, the march to Pretoria began. The Volunteers eventually caught up with them in June.

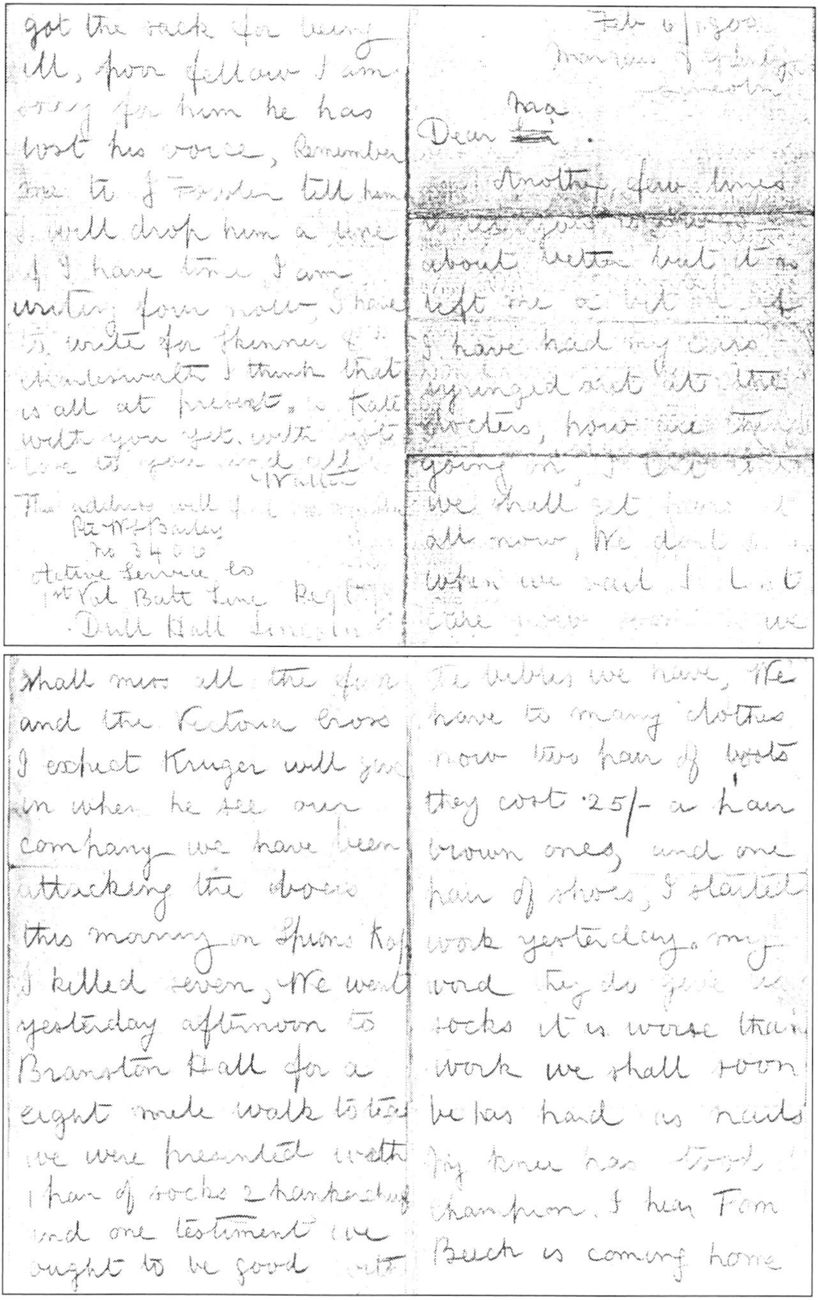

Fig. 5 Manuscript of Letter 3, dated 6 February 1900.

Lindsey and Lincolnshire Star, 24 February 1900, p. 5

LINCOLNSHIRE VOLUNTEERS OFF TO THE FRONT –
A GRAND SEND-OFF

Two Lincolnshire Volunteer Battalions left Lincoln on 17 February
amid a scene of enthusiasm unparalleled in the history of the city ...
They were not absent-minded beggars – they had not taken the
Queen's shilling.

The vast thoroughfare was packed and through the surging sea of
humanity the men had literally to fight their way ... the whole scene
was of a city gone mad ... Some of the soldiery lost their khaki
helmets ... The crowd was utterly beyond control.

For some time the train was delayed, the driver not daring to turn
on the steam, but at length a way was clear and at almost snail's pace,
the train moved out of the station.

The reference to the 'absent-minded beggar' is taken from the poem of that title
by Rudyard Kipling. It refers to the Reservist of the Regular Army who 'heard his
country's call' but left his family commitments, absent-mindedly, behind him. The
first stanza of this poem reads –

> *When you've shouted 'Rule Britannia', when you've sung 'God*
> *save the Queen',*
> *When you've finished killing Kruger with your mouth,*
> *Will you kindly drop a shilling in my little tambourine*
> *For a gentleman in khaki ordered South?*
> *He's an absent-minded beggar, and his weaknesses are great –*
> *But we and Paul must take him as we find him –*
> *He is out on active service, wiping something off a slate –*
> *And he's left a lot of little things behind him!*

Letter 4

S.S.Guelph

Dear Mother
    We have just arrived on board we sail at two. We left Lincoln at
$1/2$ past one this morning and arrived here at ten so we had a long
ride. I do not know yet where you have to write to, but will send

word when I do. Tell J Fowler we have not received the parcel, its a good job I bought some tobacco. Ben Escritt send me 18/- what he asked a few in the club for. Tell George we shall be sailers as well as soldiers, there is nearly 1000 on Board all Volunteers. I will write to Lilly and Kate when we get settled down.

I have wired to J Fowler so you will have seen it before you open this. I will write more next time. Goodbye for the present, remember me to all. Lilly sent me a photo of Baby

With best love
Walter

The *Hull Times* published a series throughout the war entitled 'War By Letter'. The following letter from Private Townsend of the Barton Volunteers, written from Tenerife, describes life on board the *Guelph*.

Hull Times, 24 March 1900, p. 11

'*It ran in my mind as we were leaving the docks at Southampton that many an anxious heart would be glad to know of or have some simple idea what sort of life our lads had to contend with; so I made up my mind just to give my experiences which no doubt will coincide with those of my comrades aboard.*'

[After referring to the hearty send-off from Lincoln and Grantham, the writer goes on to say,] '*Having safely deposited our rifles and kits on board, it was not long before "All on board" was sounded. Then began the last parting, and many a heavy heart was on the dock side as we slowly steamed away from our native land, singing many old favourite airs and concluding with "God Save the Queen". We began our journey in drizzling rain and a rather heavy wind. We sighted the Needles just an hour before we turned in. Sunday morning dawned with a gale blowing right in our teeth, just as we were entering the Bay of Biscay.*

'*Just take a look round the cabin this morning and see the havoc the gale has wrought amongst the lads. Scarce one out of 800 can scramble out of his hammock on account of seasickness. It struck me that if Her Majesty could have seen us all she would have wept. We passed Ushant Lighthouse and nothing else of interest could be seen. We did not sight a vessel until Tuesday night, when we saw a French man-of-war three miles off. Just as we turned in at eight o'clock we sighted the lighthouse off Cape Finisterre, and when we rose in the morning we received the most welcome tidings that we had cleared the Bay of Biscay, having been 65 hours struggling in a gale instead of 35 hours. What a change, too, in the lads; not one left on the sick list, everyone full of life; and from then on things began to take a more orderly routine. Rise, six o'clock; breakfast, eight, haddock, beefsteak, bread and butter and coffee; dinner, 12, soup, pork and currant roll; tea, 5.30, jam, bread and butter. The food, so far as I can judge, is wholesome and there is plenty of it. At ten o'clock we all parade at our different grounds, and are told off into first, second and third watches. A certain number from each watch are told off to clean mess rooms up, tidy hammocks and clean up generally. We are all well on board, and may look forward to a most enjoyable passage. We are twelve at a table, and all hammocks are slung at night over your own table. If you can't get it slung there, sling it somewhere else, or you have a rough time of it on the floor. We are progressing very favourably. The Atlantic is fairly calm, and we have seen several dolphins playing about the vessel's side.*

'We have just discovered there are several first class passengers on board. They have just come out after the sea sickness for a blow. Most of them are ladies and I believe several nurses, some of them for the Yeomanry.

'Ha! Ha! Ha! It's nothing much – only a small group of ladies swept on their backs by about half a ton of water, and I'm in a nice dry place.

'There's those naughty girls laughing too!

'Lemonade is 3d a bottle. All 3d – cheese and biscuits, and all sorts of groceries at special rates. We had a really good sing-song tonight. Some excellent songs were rendered by really good talent from amongst the ranks. It is a struggle to get a wash, there being about 25 basins for the lot. Breakfast is over and we are now in for half an hour's fun. The ship is rolling and our lads are trying to shave themselves and one another. Cotton wool and plaster are much in evidence, likewise the destructive work of the amateur barber.

Yours sincerely,
A Son of the Empire'

Letter 5

Feb 22nd/1900
Atlantic Ocean

Dear Ma

We are nearly again the Canary Islands now. We have passed through the Bay of Biscay and very pleased too, we had three days and three nights in it, we were nearly all sick. I recovered yesterday, I got a bottle of beer 6d and it made me well, we are only allowed one per day, small ones. They talk about waves mountains high but we had some in the Bay, it was splendid but awful, we have not had a smooth day yet. We are having the roughest voyage of any transport yet, we sometimes only have gone 1 mile per hour when it was extra rough. We are two days behind our time now. I expect we [shall] call at Teneriffe tomorrow to post our letters.

We see plenty of vessels and get plenty to eat. Breakfast, coffee, Beef steak and Herrings, Bread and butter; Dinner Roast and boiled beef, boiled and roast mutton and same pork, potatoes, all sorts of puddings; tea, Smoked Haddock and Kippers and cold meat, tea and jam or marmalade. We shall be as fat as butter soon now we have got the sickness over.

We sleep in hammocks, at night we go to bed sometimes at 6 o'clock. There is scores of us sat on deck now writing. There are two or three young fellows in the hospital on board, they gave two of them a few minutes to live this morning but I haven't heard if they are dead. It is pneumonia, with sitting on deck at sunset when the change comes in the wind, we seem to be worse without oranges and apples. Lemonade & soda 4d per bottle.

Show J Fowler this then I shan't have to write to him yet, then send it to Kate and Lilly. We have just passed the Geika with wounded and sick on board from Africa. Dont give garden up, I should get someone to do it for you if you only had peas and beans and such like. I will pay for it when we get back so goodbye.

With best love Walter
Pte W S Barley
No 6531
1 Vol Batt Linc Regt
Active Service Co
South Africa

Remember me to George and Carrie
[No of Identity Card 6531]

Hull Times, 7 April 1900, p. 9

ON THE WAY TO THE CAPE

Private T. Hockney, a Scunthorpe Volunteer with the Lincolns, writing to his father Mr T. Hockney, Mary-street, on March 7th, off St Helena, says:–

'At Teneriffe there was any amount of fruit to be had, and we enjoyed ourselves but we were not allowed off the ship. The natives brought plenty round. You could get tobacco at a shilling per pound, and cigars at 2s a hundred. We got a good stock in. We have all got tanned, and don't look like the same men now. Our captain says we shall be coming back in April, but we have no war news since we left Teneriffe, so don't know how they are going on. We have sports two or three times a week on board and concerts every night.'

Letter 6

This letter, given to me by May, is incomplete.

… of flying fishes, dolpins, porpoises, nautillus and one albatross. A dove settled on the ship yesterday it was easily caught. We have all had to make our wills. I made mine to you, with Mr Fowler as executor. Are you getting the money, you have never said a word about it.

I expect we shall have to rough it when we leave the ship, we have never been better fed in our lives. One of those fellows died, he was one of the Yorks, they sold all his clothes to send the money home. His knife made 10/- so they made something for them.

Remember me to all. Send this to Kate and Lillie. Ask George how the dancing goes, we don't get any here, we have plenty of concerts instead. I think I shall have to conclude, it is morning and they are coming for the letters at half past seven.

With best love
Walter

Letter 7

> Dear Lillie and Kate
> Charlie and Harry
>   You can read this I have sent Mother. I am going on champion. I
> hope you all are. We shall come home again in a few months time.
> Give the children a kiss for me and tell them I will bring something
> from Africa for them if I don't get spent up, tell them I will get them a
> little black boy. Tell Charlie I shall want that gallon of Beer when I
> come, from the Blue Anchor, tell the Landlord
> > > With best love
> > > Walter

MEANWHILE ...[2]

December 1899 to 16 March 1900

In December, while Walter and his fellow Volunteers were going through the selection procedures for active service and, in the New Year, being assessed and trained
at Grantham and Lincoln prior to embarkation, the British Army in South Africa
was coming to terms with the disasters of Black Week, and the sieges of the towns
of Kimberley, Mafeking and Ladysmith.

These and other reverses, including the failure of General Sir Redvers Buller,
the Commander-in-Chief, to relieve Ladysmith, led on 18 December to the
appointment in London of Frederick, Lord Roberts, the hero of the Indian Mutiny,
to succeed Buller. Accompanied by Lord Kitchener as Chief of Staff, Roberts
embarked for South Africa on 23 December and was expected in Cape Town on
11 January.

Buller, rather than await orders, decided to renew the attempt to relieve
Ladysmith by crossing the Tugela River and embarking on a flanking movement
towards the town. Taking and crossing the mountains, the most prominent peak
of which was Spion Kop, now spelt 'Spioen Kop' in South Africa, meaning 'Look-
out Hill', was crucial. Despite an early success in capturing the Kop, the ensuing
battle was lost by a series of miscalculations and lack of accurate intelligence and
cost the British 1,500 men dead, wounded and captured. It also cost Buller his military reputation, earning for him – as he was forced to retreat across the Tugela –
the nickname of Reverse Buller.

By the time the Lincolnshire Volunteers embarked on the *Guelph*, Roberts, affectionately known to the troops as 'Bobs', had arrived to take up his command. Ever impatient, he decided to leave Buller in Natal without reinforcements, and himself, with five divisions of 40,000 men, begin the 'steamroller' advance to capture Bloemfontein, the capital of the Orange Free State, and to relieve the diamond town of Kimberley where Cecil Rhodes was trapped. Frustrated by the slowness of the accompanying supply columns, Roberts made certain rash changes in the transport system and thereby denied the army adequate food and drinking water, as well as medical supplies and services. This situation was made worse when, on 15 February, Christiaan De Wet, never slow to seize an opportunity, captured 200 unprotected supply wagons at Waterfal Drift on the Riet River.

Major-General John French, who, wisely, had retained his own transport, made a dash for Kimberley and successfully relieved the town on 15 February. The Boer commander, General Piet Cronje, retreated along the railway line to join De Wet and was engaged by Kitchener at the costly but inconclusive Battle of Paardeberg, in which most of the rashly engaged British cavalry was lost. When Roberts arrived De Wet withdrew and, on 27 February, a demoralised Cronje with over four thousand men surrendered. On the same day Buller at last succeeded in opening the road to Ladysmith and relieved it on the 18th. Walter's friend 'Lockey', Arthur Lockwood of the 19th Hussars, reached Ladysmith soon after the relief and, in his letters home, described the parlous state of the town.

As the transport *Guelph* approached the Cape, Roberts was pushing on towards Bloemfontein. The Boer Army was engaged at Poplar Grove on 7 March, but the British advantage was not followed up and the Boers slipped away. President Kruger, who was with the Boer commando, managed to escape. When Bloemfontein was taken with surprising ease on 13 March, Roberts found that the Boer commandos had fled. He assumed, wrongly as it turned out, that Boer resistance was broken and the war nearly over. He therefore offered amnesty to all those, except the leaders, who would lay down their arms.

The Lincolnshire Volunteers arrived in Cape Town on 15 March and within four days were on their way to Tulbagh to guard the railway. It was here that a copy of the Bloemfontein newspaper *The Friend* of 15 March, found among Walter's papers, must have come into his hands. In it were Roberts's amnesty proclamations to the Boers, which gave rise to the belief among the fighting men that the war was all but over.[3]

Chapter 4

Cape Town to Tulbagh

March to April 1900

> *The twilight swallows the thicket,*
>   *The starlight reveals the ridge;*
> *The whistle shrills to the picket –*
>   *We are changing guard on the bridge.*

> *(Few, forgotten and lonely,*
>   *Where the empty metals shine –*
> *No, not combatants – only*
>   *Details guarding the line.)*

> Kipling – 'Bridge Guard in the Karoo'

When the transport *Guelph* arrived at Cape Town, neither Walter nor Tom Hockney, who wrote home at the same time, commented on the magnificent landfall in Table Bay or on the scenic beauty of the Cape Peninsula. The Volunteers spent only four days at Cape Town and, as Walter reported to his mother, two of these were spent on the transport.

Lindsey and Lincolnshire Star, 14 April 1900, p. 5

LETTER FROM A VOLUNTEER

Private Tom Hockney at Green Point, Cape Town
'We arrived at Cape Town on Friday, 16 March. Some ladies came on

39

board and gave us grapes and wine. I don't think we shall be in South Africa long. We saw all the Boer prisoners that have been sent off to St. Helena.'

Private W.S. Barley who wrote home about the same time, said that he had seen George Fields of Scunthorpe who was recovering from a wound.

As several letters from Walter to his mother appear in either the *Lindsey and Lincolnshire Star* or the *Hull Times*, sometimes in both, it is obvious that Mrs Barley passed the letter on to a reporter friend of the family, presumably the H. Dickinson whom Walter mentions in his letters.

Letter 8

Tulbagh
March 20 1900

Dear Mother

Just a line or two to let you know how I am. We are roughing it now, Bully Beef and biscuits. We arrived at Cape Town all right and laid in Table Bay two days, then we camped at Green Point, just off Cape Town. They were making ready for Boer prisoners. We stayed there two days, and were pleased to get out, there was so much sand, ten times worse than Aldershot. We saw G Fields there, he had been wounded in the thigh, he showed us the wound, he is better now.

We left Cape Town Sunday morning and arrived at Tulbagh late at night, putting our tents up at dark. If it had been at camp we should have been swearing but here we take it as a matter of course. We are camped in a valley about thirty or forty miles circumferance with mountains all round us, there are hundreds of monkeys on the mountains. Nearly all the men are away fighting, as Tulbagh is mostly Boers, it is about 100 miles from Cape Town. Tell G King we have seen his sister and her husband several times, tell him I knew the face at once.

I shall have to conclude, has our tent is going on guard tonight to guard some bridge 15 miles off from the Boers, we go with 100 rounds of ammunition each man. Send this to Sheffield. We captured a Boer the other night rolling Boulders off the mountain on the railway.

With love Walter

Tom Hockney wrote again to his parents from Tulbagh Road on 27 March. His letter was published in the *Hull Times* in the 'War By Letter' series.

Hull Times, 28 April 1900, p. 9

'We are camping at Tulbagh-road station and we have been here since we left Cape Town 150 miles away. Its a fine country, but there is nothing to see where we are, as there are only about a dozen houses. The village is four miles away and we go three times a week. There is only one Englishman in the place. Most of them are Boers. They don't trouble us much. We are most of our time looking after the railway. We have two stations to look after, 15 miles apart by train. We have eight or nine big bridges to look after. It is all night work. The railway men look after them in the day. We have only two nights a week to do. We do very little drilling. There are a lot of troops guarding the line up here, all Volunteers, and we have plenty of games.

'They sent us footballs from Cape Town. We get fresh meat and bread every morning from the same place. All the troops and stores go through here, we see them all, and all the prisoners. We always know when they are coming as we guard the station. They sometimes try to get out, but we shoot them if they do. I don't think we shall get any further up country just yet.'

Letter 9

Tulbagh
April 1/00

Dear Mother

We are getting sick of being shut up here, we might has well be at home and there seems no chance of moving. It is all hard work, 8 mile walk each morning before breakfast so we are ready for it when we get back. We have to carry 100 rounds of ammunition and they get heavy before we get back. After breakfast bathing parade, another three miles then dinner, then drill in the afternoon about $1^1/_2$ hours in the blazing sun without our coats, running about in the bushes.

The officers have put the hotel out of bounds but we manage to sneak a drink but it is risky. The Cape Town Highlanders are here and they get 3 barrels in at once so we go to their camp. We see hundreds of troops come through and train loads of wounded and prisoners too, one jumped out of the train on the side of our camp, we are close to the line, he escaped, was shot and buried in 15 minutes, quick work that. The Yeomanry are camped four mile off here, we see them nearly every day.

It is a regular hot bed for Boers here. We don't see many young ones, these are all away fighting, we are here to keep them quiet. We march on different roads every day, they do look nasty at us, some of them wont sell us anything. The niggers bring us milk in a morning, 3d a pint, it is better than English. We get a pound of meat, 1 loaf and coffee per day, jam twice a week, no butter, dry bread and coffee, its nice with sand thrown in. I think we have eaten our share of it now. In our soup at dinnertime ants is always on the top, piss mires as we call them at home.

I have never received a letter while we have been here, all the other fellows have, don't you write. We have just been to Church Parade but the Parson did not turn up so we sang God Save the Queen. Send this to Sheffield to them, I am writing this on my mess tin for a table. We have to climb a mountain once a week, it takes three hours so you know how big they are.

Love to all Walter

Private Fred Skinner of K Company wrote to his parents from Tulbagh Camp on 3 April. It has so many similarities to the letter written by Walter on 1 April that it seems likely that Walter was still writing Fred's letters for him, as he had reported earlier.

Hull Times, 15 May 1900, p. 9, in the 'War By Letter' series

FRODINGHAM VOLUNTEER ON SOUTH AFRICAN SCENES

'We arrived at Cape Town all right and camped at Green Point, with about 10,000. It was an awful place for sand. We had sand storms all the time. We saw the guns there that they captured from Cronje.

'We left there on the Sunday, so we have been here nearly three weeks. We are here to keep things quiet, as it is a hot place for Boers.

'There is an hotel here, but the officers have put it out of bounds, so we can't get any. We have got to know what hard work is (eight mile route march every morning before breakfast), so we are ready for something to eat when we get back. Bathing parade before dinner, then another three *miles. In the afternoon another 1½ hour's drill in the blazing sun. For meals – Breakfast and tea, dry bread, coffee and sand; dinner, boiled mutton or beef. Jam twice a week. We have four bridges to guard, two of them about 15 miles off. There have been two men killed there. It is a lonely place. We see hundreds of troops go through, as well as prisoners. One jumped out of the carriage against our camp. He was shot and a grave dug and him buried in 15 minutes. That's quick, wasn't it?*

'Our Captain had a wire from Lord Roberts last night to be ready to join the regiment at an early date. We are ready. We are tired of being here.

'It is a valley with mountains all round us, about 40 miles round. We have to climb the mountains once a week. It takes about three hours to do it, so you can guess how big they are.'

Private Skinner sends home four Kaffir necklaces, similar to those worn by the Kaffir women. They are quite a curiosity, and are in bright colours. They appear to be made of melon and other seeds, and are very neatly put together. The beads were sent home in a cocoa tin.

Letter 10

Tulbagh
April 3/1900

Dear Lillie

Just a line or two to tell you we are going to the front shortly. Our Captain had a wire last night, from Lord Roberts to hold ourselves in readiness to join the Regiment at an early date. I wrote to Mother on Sunday so did not tell her about it.

I have nothing fresh to tell you as I expect Mother sends you her letters. It is a blazing hot day here, sweat pouring down our faces as we are writing these letters, then we have 1½ hours drill in it with all coats off. You would not know us, what with being sunburnt and our whiskers on. There is one thing about it we never enjoyed better health in our lives before, we can eat like horses, even dry bread and water.

I think there will only be one more battle now and it will be over, the worst of it we can't get much beer. Tell Charlie I shall want that gallon from the public when we get back. We shall get a medal now, wont it look nice on Church Parade, but we should like to earn it in fighting. We have earned one I think in hard work.

Kiss the bairns for me. The bugle is just going for parade so goodbye for the present with love to all. Walter

Hull Times, 19 May 1900, p. 9

LINCS. VOLUNTEERS 'GROWING FAT'

*Private Thomas Hockney, one of the Scunthorpe Volunteers, writing
to his parents at Scunthorpe from Tulbagh-road Station, Cape Colony,
on April 8th, says:–*
   'We look a nice lot now. We have not had a shave since we
landed, and our whiskers look lovely. They are talking of taking us a
bit higher up the country, but we don't know when we go. We have
been ready a fortnight. We are tired of being here guarding the
railway, there is nothing to see but a few niggers. This country agrees
with us, and we are all getting fat.'

Letter 11

April 10th/1900
Tulbagh

Dear Mother
   We are still at Tulbagh. I wrote a week since, six letters to
different people. I don't know whether you will get any, has the
Mexican went down and some of the mails went down with her.
   Me and Skinner went on Sunday to the Yeomanry Camp about 12
miles, we walked there and back. They entertained us to tea, salmon
and jam, then we had two buckets of beer among us all, which went
down very well. The things are dear here, salmon 1/- a tin, cheese 1/6
per pound, sugar 7d, tobacco is cheap 1d per oz. I get two oz for 3d,
cigarettes 6d a packet. Tell Mr Fowler we have not received any
tobacco, we want it too as we are spent up and have to wait while the
end of the month before we get paid.
   We are nearly always on guard 24 hours at a time, and have to do
the 8 mile march before we go on, only half an hour rest between for
breakfast so we are working strong, but we are in splendid health, I
don't think I have been better in my life. I expect it is with having
bathes every morning, they freshen us up a treat, they all have to go
whether they want or not. We have a march tomorrow in full
marching order, that means about 45lb extra to carry, that fetches the
sweat out. We get plenty to eat if it is only bread and coffee.
   I wrote to Sheffield to them but I expect it has gone down in the
Mexican same as yours has. I have never received a letter since I left

England from nowhere. We have only got one Hull Times too, we get papers from Cape Town every day but the news is always late, they have to get their news from England. I think that is all, as I don't want to write what I put in the other letter for perhaps you might get it. Tell George that Ted Ball is here with us from Lincoln, he says he knows him. Remember me to all, with best love

Walter

Letter 12

April 17th 1900
Tulbagh

Dear Mother

We are still at Tulbagh and dont see any likelihood of going any farther. All the Volunteers that came in the same boat have gone to the front but us. Troops keep coming past in hundreds. I think G Hughes is at Cape Town as the Guards are there, I have not heard anything of A Lockwood. I should think he will have gone to Durban.

On Good Friday we had bathing Parade at seven, then breakfast, we bought some hot cross buns, the storekeeper ordered 500 from Cape Town they were 2d each. Then we had another parade, then dinner, in the afternoon we went fishing as we had half a day holiday. We caught a few, they are something like our roach. At night we had to go to Breeda Bridges, 15 mile off, to guard them.

On Sunday we had a heavy storm, poured all day, the rainy season is coming on now, you dont see storms in England like them. I was orderly for our tent so I got wet through as we have to go half a mile to fetch drinking water. If we hadnt had trenches dug round the tent we should have been flooded out.

On Easter Monday we had a route march, and drilled same as other days they was no holiday for us, then I had to go on guard again for 24 hours, it is nearly all guard I think. I was pleased I was on, as today they are going on a twenty mile march, they went out at seven and we came off at ten so we miss it champion.

I have to take plenty of salts here, the beer here binds me instead of working me, its a good job they keep them. I have had a couple of days off. I told them my back was bad so I got off. A Charlesworth told me about Cooper breaking. I should think he will go to America now.

If you get that letter that was on board the Mexican keep it has it will be a curiosity with being shipwrecked. I expect all our letters and things go to Bloemfontein to the Regiment has we don't get any. We have played two football matches with the Cape Town Highlanders, the first was a draw, second we won 7 to 1. We are all in splendid health, send this to Sheffield.

With love to all and you,

Walter

Tell Charlie or Harry to save my knife, as it is a particular favourite

Walter's surmise that his friend Arthur Lockwood, 'Lockey', had gone to Natal was proved correct. His unit had arrived at Ladysmith after the town was relieved on 28 February. The following letters appeared in the *Hull Times* on 12 May 1900, p. 9.

SCUNTHORPE RESERVIST AT LADYSMITH

Trooper Arthur Lockwood, of the 19th Hussars, a Scunthorpe reservist, writing to his father, Mr R.D. Lockwood, architect, under dates 28th March and 4th April from Ladysmith, says:–

'We arrived safe after a rough voyage. We were just five weeks getting to Ladysmith. We stopped there one day, and then moved eight miles on the other side. We are only 10 miles from the front and can hear the guns firing every day. We have several Boer prisoners.

'The men that were at Ladysmith all look bad. My regiment lost while they were besieged in Ladysmith 84 men. They had 354 horses when they went into Ladysmith, and when they came out they had only 75, they had eaten the others. The men say they would sooner shoot themselves than go through the same again.

'General Buller came into camp on Monday, and had a look round. He has had a hard job to get where he is. They are the biggest hills I ever saw. Our lot are having a rest, but we might go at any time. It would only take about three hours to get to the front. We are on biscuits and bully beef. We think it a treat to have a good feed of biscuits. They are biscuits too; as hard as iron! We get bread tomorrow.

'You cannot buy anything in Ladysmith, as all the shops are closed. It is only a small place. We saw where the Boers shelled the places and blew the tower off the Town Hall. Men go out every night to patrol the country. I slept two nights out in the open. I met George Dinsdale of

Scunthorpe in Durban, and was with him about three hours.

'We lost 20 horses coming out, they knocked about so. This is a nice country, everything green and no dust much. It would take us half a day to go up some of the big hills, they are so rough and stony. The barbed wire is all over the country for miles, and you can't see it until you are on top of it, owing to the long grass.

'I saw the bridges that the Boers blew up. They were just burying General Woodgate at Mooi River as we passed in the train. I saw Lieutenant Robert's grave and hundreds of others.'

'I had a touch of dysentery last week, but am getting better. I have been with the 13th Hussars two days up at the front. I had to go out with 250 of our men on night duty. They fired at us but didn't hit anybody.

'The Boers are like rabbits, and are very artful. They don't fire until you get on top of them.'

Lieutenant Freddy Roberts, the only son of Lord Roberts, was killed at the Battle of Colenso on 15 December 1899. Major-General E.R.P. Woodgate, the Commanding Officer of the Lancashire Brigade, whose burial was witnessed by Lockey, was wounded at the Battle of Spion Kop on 24 January 1900 and died soon after.

Letter 13

Tulbagh
April 22 1900

Dear Mother

I received a letter from Kate, April 18th, it was dated 10 March. I expect it had been to Bloemfontein to the Regiment, and one from Ada Cherrill from Lincoln, Mrs Pearts neice. I went to see them when we were at Lincoln and had tea there.

It is five weeks today Sunday we have been at Tulbagh, since we have been here we have marched about 350 miles, a nice stretch, my boots is about the best in the company. I am going to buy a card of protectors tomorrow to mend them with, nearly all the others have had to have them mended. They have to march to the village 4 miles off to get them done. My word they know how to charge, for two caps on the toes 5/-, for a patch on the heel 1/6, six protectors 8d and we have to pay it out of our own pocket, it is a bit thick.

The fellows are playing football now, as I am writing this, this afternoon we are going fishing again to try and get a fry. Lady Roberts passed through the station one night this week for Bloemfontein. We got a snake 6 feet long and only as thick as my walking stick. We catch a snake and a scorpion, put them under a box and they fight sometimes to the death. The scorpions are like spiders with claws like crabs, the sting is at the end of their tails which curls over their backs, they cant sting underneath only when you touch their backs. The centipedes are like caterpillers with millions of legs. When they crawl on you they stick their legs in, it makes your flesh look like a big weal. The lizards are harmless they are like little crocodiles, we pick them up, they live on insects.

I was sorry to hear about Ned Dallas getting hurt. I hope you enjoyed your spice cake, shall you make one when I come back. I expect when Lord Roberts makes a move it will soon be over. The Yeomanry keep going up, they are getting mounted troops up there quick now, so there will have been some heavy fighting before you get this.

I saw my letter in Chit Chat in Hull Times. It is a sight to see the greedy look on the mens faces when letters come and the downcast look when there is none, same as I have been fixed, it is a red letter day when they come. We have 50 men on guard every other night so you see we have some places to guard.

We are going to Ceres again on Tuesday, there is some splendid moths there, about six inches across the wings. I should like to make a collection of them but we havent time. It is a rare thing to see a horse in a cart, they run from two to 18, either horses, mules or oxen. The fourth Middlesex past here yesterday on a route march about 800 of them, with a band playing, that sounded like England, I should like to stop here, they get about 20 or 30£ a month higher up. You can tell how hot it is here sometimes while the wax candles bend double.

We often get baskets of Grapes sent us sometimes 3 or 4 lb a man. We would sooner have apples they are splendid here, and watermelons, they are simply grand. I expect we shall have a rare fuddle when we get home. I shall be thirty before you get this, a week tomorrow, it is 5 weeks since I had a shave so you may guess I look well.

There are some pretty birds here, and hares rabbits and pheasants, the rabbits will bite like dogs, they have feet like monkeys for climbing and no tails. How is George getting on, tell him Kopjes is pronounced copies. Have you got anybody to do a bit of gardening has I shant get home in time. I shall want some kidney beans and marrows when I come. I hope we get home in time for camp, it is over three months to so we might manage it.

Remember me to all, tell Mr Fowler there is nothing startling to tell him or I would write, send this to Sheffield. Kiss baby for me, May I mean.

With love to you and all

Walter

The strange rabbit described by Walter was almost certainly the dassie (*Procavia capensis*), sometimes known as a rock rabbit but not related to the rabbit family. It can be identified as the biblical coney.

Walter also wrote letters to other contacts in Scunthorpe, although he often used the same material as in his letters to his mother. The one below was published in the Hull Times on 19 May 1900.

SCUNTHORPE MAN ON SOUTH AFRICAN CAMP LIFE

Private W.S. Barley, one of the Scunthorpe Volunteers, writing from Tulbagh, April 24th, to our Scunthorpe reporter, says:–
'We are camped at Tulbagh Station, about four miles from the village and about 100 miles from Cape Town. It is a lively hole, about a dozen houses. We are on the line of communication, guarding four bridges. Two of them are about 15 miles off. We always carry 100 rounds of ammunition with us. We do some hard work – eight mile walk every morning before breakfast. We have a splendid bathing place. We go every morning before dinner. I expect it is that which is making us so healthy. We go fishing on Sunday afternoons or else play football. Last Sunday we caught 62 fish, 3 crabs and 2 frogs so we had a good fry.

'I saw my letter in the Hull Times. I was sorry to see Ned Dallas had got hurt. We have a lot of enemies here, viz., snakes, centipedes, scorpions, lizards, etc. We have killed many a lot. The biggest snake we killed was 6ft long. We catch the small ones and put them into a box with a scorpion, and then we have some fun. They fight to the death. A scorpion is like a spider, with claws like a crab. Its sting is in its tail, and they can use them.

'The mountains are a tremendous height here. It takes three hours to go up and down. There are scores of monkeys on them. The kopjes

*are pronounced "copies". We are camped at the foot of Kloof Kop.
We received some papers and letters yesterday. I also got a box of
cigarettes from A. Wigfall but J. Fowler's tobacco has not reached me
yet. I posted half-a-dozen letters by the Mexican, so I suppose they
have gone down.'*

Letter 14

Tulbagh
April 23 1900

Dear Mother

I wrote the other letter yesterday so put this in to let you know I
got the cigarettes today, I hadnt got any to smoke so they came in
nice. The Tobacco has not come yet. You will be having a bank book
now, I should think you will be rich when I come home. I saw in the
paper you were getting off rates and taxes, that is a good job. I am
pleased George is going to do the garden. Give mine and Alicks best
thanks to Mr Fowler for what he has done.

good night
with best love
Walter

Walter celebrated his thirtieth birthday at Tulbagh on 30 April. He must have
valued the card sent to him by his sister, Lillie, as he sent it back for safe keeping.
The card was not, however, found among his letters and papers.

Letter 15

Tulbagh
April 29 1900

Dear Mother

I received a letter from Lillie with a birthday card last night. I
have sent it back else it would get torn here. We went on a twenty
four mile march yesterday to Ceres, the prettiest place here. Tell Lillie
to send you the letter, I have sent her a description of it so it is no use
writing it so many times.

We are still at Tulbagh, our Captain keeps saying we are going up
but I dont know when. Troops are constantly going through but here

we stop so we shall have to rest contented. We had a treat last Thursday, a man in the village sent some cabbages, we did enjoy them.

I dont know what to write about there is nothing fresh here, it is the same routine every day. We go down to the Highlanders Camp every night and have a sing song, they have a couple of Irish men there, they do keep us alive. We have not got the tobacco yet, if he addressed it to Skinner we might not get it as there is another Skinner with the Regiment. Tell George to set the potatoes right way up and plant some marrows. Have you put some water in the paints and brushes else they will spoil. Tell Trueman I will play him when I get back, but I shall want some start has I havent seen a billiard here.

I sent Lillie a few sprigs of heather, it was all I got on the march. She asked me to send a bit. Ask baby if she will come to see her uncle in a puffer train, give her a kiss for me.

Remember me to all enquirers.

With love
Walter

Letter 16

April 28th/1900
Tulbagh

Dear Lillie

I received your letter late on Saturday night, we had just come off a twenty four mile march. Thanks for the Birthday Card, I am sending it back has it will only get broke here, we have nowhere to keep anything. I am sending you a sprig or two of heather.

We had a splendid march yesterday to Ceres. The villages are between ten and twenty miles off the stations, Tulbagh Road or Ceres Road and so on. Well we took train at seven oclock all in one truck about forty feet long and rode to Ceres Road about fifteen mile, then we marched. We saw some splendid scenery, some of the best in South Africa, it looks like a lie but it was ten miles uphill. We started at the bottom of the mountain and reached the top before we got to the village. It was a good road, mountains on the left and on the right, precipices from 500 to 1000 ft down, it made one dizzy to look down. There were waterfalls in abundance, the palms and ferns were very pretty. What we have in Greenhouses in England grows wild here.

We were repaid for our walk when we got there, the way we were entertained. The magistrate or Landroost met us and took us into the park. We had tea, biscuits and cheese, beer, stout and lemonade. Ceres is supposed to be the prettiest village down here. I cant decribe it because I cant do it justice, there are only 13 loyal families in it. When we started home downhill we marched the first six mile in an hour, our Captain congratulated us on our marching powers, we are going again shortly to stop the night. I stood it well except a bit of chafing.

We have not got any further orders yet about going to the front, but the Captain keeps saying we are going. We all keep in splendid health, the climate just suits us, except being cold at nights, it gets dark here in about 10 minutes. We have fifteen in our tent so we are nicely packed has we have only eight in at camp. I hope we get back in time to go, we sleep on the ground on a waterproof and one blanket to cover us.

I shall come and spend a week if I get back all right. I was a bit inquisitive about the Garden but Mother says that George is going to do it so thats all right. I told her I wanted some marrows and kidney beans. We had a treat last Thursday, we had some cabbage given us. Kiss the children for me. Tell Ada I will come back.

With love to all

Walter

MEANWHILE ...

20 March to 30 April 1900

While the Volunteers were guarding the railway line at Tulbagh about a hundred miles from Cape Town, Roberts and his large force were stalled at Bloemfontein. The intention had been to move rapidly forward into the Transvaal to capture Johannesburg and Pretoria, but various factors caused the army to delay. The most telling of these, in which Roberts was supported by Alfred Milner, was the fear that, if attacked, the Boers would carry out their threat to blow up the gold mines and thus rob the colonial power of their main economic objective.

The condition of the army in Bloemfontein was an additional factor in the delay. The British garrison was isolated and overcrowded. Supplies depended on the single-track railway line from the Cape which was subject to frequent Boer attacks, leaving both food and water in short supply. The insanitary camp conditions and an acute shortage of medical supplies and nurses meant that typhoid and other enteric diseases were taking a heavy toll. In addition, the cavalry and mounted infantry units were woefully short of mounts. Not only had the horses suffered in battle, as at Paardeberg, but many had endured the severe conditions on the long sea journey reported by Arthur Lockwood, and on the long march from the Cape. They needed time to recover, but fodder was in short supply and the 'unsalted' animals were prone to diseases from which they lacked immunity. The death toll, for the whole war, of horses and mules was later estimated to be in excess of forty thousand. Later in the war, the Boers were also short of mounts.[4]

Although Roberts was forced to accept that the parlous state of the army made it difficult to press on into the Transvaal, he was also firmly convinced that the amnesty offered to the Boers would work and lead to a negotiated settlement. While, however, the delay continued the Boers were slipping away and forming small fighting groups on both sides of the British lines. On 17 March a Boer Council of War was called at Kroonstad at which De Wet counselled that guerrilla tactics should be adopted with the intention of breaking the amnesty, boosting Boer morale and harrying British lines of communication. To achieve this, De Wet urged that the commandos should be formed into disciplined fighting units with the use of supply wagons minimised to increase mobility, even though this meant that the commandos would have to live off the land or on what they could capture from the British. De Wet carried the day, but the commandos proved reluctant to abandon their wagons.

The first major success of De Wet's strategy came on 31 March when he crept up on the garrison at the waterworks at Sannah's Post on the Modder River, 23 miles from Bloemfontein. Major-General R.G. Broadwood was taken prisoner along with guns, wagons and 428 men. The captured men, with those taken soon after when the garrison at Reddersburg surrendered to De Wet, were held in camp on the racecourse at Pretoria until the town fell to the British on 5 June.

It was not until the beginning of May that Roberts was ready and able to leave Bloemfontein and resume the march on Pretoria.

Chapter 5

'Marching to Pretoria'

May to July 1900

> We're foot – slog – slog – sloggin' over Africa!
> Foot – foot – foot – foot – sloggin' over Africa –
> (Boots – boots – boots – boots, movin' up and down again!)
> There's no discharge in the war!
>
> Seven – six – eleven – five – nine-an'-twenty mile to-day –
> Four – eleven – seventeen – thirty-two the day before –
> (Boots – boots – boots – boots, movin' up and down again!)
> There's no discharge in the war!
>
> Kipling – 'Boots (Infantry Columns of the Earlier War)'

As Roberts's army left Bloemfontein, the Volunteers received orders to leave Tulbagh and begin the journey to join their regiment. They travelled by rail as far as Brandfort but a few miles further on a bridge had been blown up and they had to leave the train. The rest of the distance to Pretoria was made in forced marches in record time. They caught up with their regiment at Kroonstad in the north of the Orange Free State and marched with them into the Transvaal.

The stages by which the 2nd Lincolns had reached Kroonstad, and the battles fought on the way, were recorded in the *Hull Times* in the words of one of the soldiers, Private E. King. King got no further than Kroonstad as he was wounded in the battle for the town and invalided home.

Hull Times, 21 July 1900, p. 7

LINCOLNSHIRE SOLDIER'S EXCITING EXPERIENCES

On Tuesday, while waiting at Barnetby Station, a 'Times' representative got into conversation with Private E. King, 2nd Lincolns, who was on his way to Caistor, being invalided home. His regiment was stationed at Lincoln and the commanding officer was Col. Roberts, unfortunately wounded and captured at Nitral's Nek. They embarked on the Ghoorka on January 4th and landed at Cape Town on January 27th. After remaining there a few days the march to Pretoria was begun. King, however, was not destined to see the march completed, and according to his own account, must have had a rough time.

King took part in engagements at Poplar Grove, Keere, Brandford, Bloemfontein, Paardeberg and Kroonstad. He was present at Paardeberg when Cronje surrendered, and was one of those who bade farewell to the noted Boer leader when he left for St Helena. At this time they were living on a biscuit and a half per day, and the water they had to drink was taken from the Modder River, at the time when dead Boers and dead horses were polluting the river.

King got no further than Kroonstad, for here their progress was challenged by a number of the enemy. It was only after a battle existing from 6 a.m. to 5.30 p.m. that they gained victory and resumed the march. King received a bullet through the fleshy part of the right thigh, and was detained in the Dutch Hospital 15 days. After this he was sent down to Cape Town in No 2 Hospital Train and detained in hospital a further 21 days. He sailed in the Armenian, and last Tuesday reached Grimsby, where he has a brother living. He speaks in terms of praise of the kindness of Colonel Roberts, and in reply to a question as to whether he would like to go back, replied, 'No, I have no strong desire to do so.'

Colonel Roberts was the Commanding Officer of the 2nd Lincolns and should not be confused with Lord Roberts.

Letter 17

De Aar Junction
May 5th

Dear Mother

On my birthday we had a good time at camp. The Yeomanry came to play us at football, we made a draw one each, after the match we entertained them to tea. Our tent No 1 had the finest spread, we took the biscuit, we all put 1/- each. To 15 of us we had salmon, sardines, jam, butter, sausages and buns, a nice spread for here, we enjoyed ourselves. On Wednesday night we were entertained to a supper by the Station Master & friends. We had a barrel of beer which went down very well. On Thursday we left Tulbagh for Bloemfontein. We have now started on Bully beef and biscuits which are harder than ship biscuits.

We shall not get there before Sunday night so we are having a long ride, but we are enjoying it has we have comfortable beds to sleep in, six in a carriage, then we have a corridor and balcony to walk on, not like our rotten carriages. We are seeing some splendid scenery, the railway through the mountains passes is marvellous, it looks impossible for man to make it, the curves are round as an apple, and you are on tops of precipices hundreds of feet high, on a sudden curve the carriages are half over.

We have just been through the Great Karroo Desert. We are leaving the large mountains behind us now and coming to more level country. We are 318 mile off Bloemfontein as I am writing this. It is 751 off Cape Town. We are getting tea and coffee three times a day at the stations. The Lancashire Volunteers are in the same train as us. We expect marching from Bloemfontein to Brandfort where our regiment is, so we expect to see a bit of something now. I hope when we get there our tobacco is waiting for us.

I heard Smith the photographer had failed, I expected it. I dont know when you will get another letter if we go up, but I will write if possible. Address letters as before, it will find our regiment, so goodbye for the present, remember me to all, send this to Sheffield. I have just got shaved first time in seven weeks, I had a good beard. Goodbye

With love
Walter

Letter 18

Brandfort
May 10/1900

We got the tobacco, it is the best in the camp. Thank Mr Fowler for us all

Dear Mother

We arrived at Bloemfontein on Sunday all right. We had a beautiful tea for Sunday night, bully beef, biscuits and cold water. My word it is a camp, theres thousands of soldiers and the stores are tremendous.

We left there on Monday night for Brandfort at 12 oclock, we had to ride on the top of a luggage train, it took us six hours, the cold was intense, we were nearly all starved through. We were on outpost duty last night about a mile out of camp, we were in twos on that duty. Me and Alec Charlesworth were together. We go out on the mountains, where they had a battle and get perched up on the kopjes, out of sight and keep a sharp look out over the veldt, to see the enemy does not get up. Where we were stationed was among a lot of dead horses and mules, they did smell strong. About 100 yds off us were the graves w[h]ere about 200 boers are buried.

We have been looking round on the kopjes and found several pieces of shells and mauser cartridges, I shall try to bring some home. There were some convoys went through yesterday, they started at six in the morning and was going through all day, they would be about 20 mile long and then Kruger thinks he can win. Why they dare not stand, every time our troops get up to them, off they go. I am nearly sure by you get this the war will be over, has our troops is on the borders of the Transvaal, they have about cleared the Free States now.

We are sleeping with the heavens for a roof now, it is cold only one blanket. I dont know how long it is since we had our clothes off except for a bathe. We havent a very good place here, we cant swim in it. The men that were here first had to drag the water to pull the dead horses and mules out, so it is a pretty place, but there is one consolation we get champion drinking water and that is the main thing. There is no beer here and we are better without it has it is so hot here.

We understand that we are going to move either tonight or tomorrow, but I dont think we can catch our regiment by marching. It is 100 miles higher up, and we can only go about 12 miles by train has the bridge is blown up over the Vet River, they are repairing it now. Two Volunteer companies left here yesterday to go and help the Engineers to repair it. I hope we dont have to go and turn into navvies for 1/3 per day.

I am very fortunate in finding salts when I could not get any. I took some soap pills, so I am keeping myself open and then I need not fear the fever.

With love to all and yourself
Walter

There follows a news clipping from the Scrapbook of the Lincolnshire Regiment in the Museum of Lincolnshire Life, Lincoln. 'Military Intelligence from Our Special Correspondent', 7 June 1900. No source quoted.

WITH THE LINCOLNS: VOLUNTEERS JOIN THE BATTALION

Kroonstad 21 May 1900
'Just a line to inform you that our Volunteer Company arrived last night. They marched about 40 miles in 24 hours and looked very fit after that long march. They are, indeed, a fine body of men [Fig. 6] and will, I feel certain, reflect credit on the Regiments to which they belong. They were this morning inspected by Gen. Maxwell who was well pleased with their appearance, and they certainly merited the encomiums passed on them by Col. Roberts. We start tomorrow for the Transvaal and will not stop until we have set foot firmly on the soil which will soon be British and Boer no more.'

Letter 19

Pretoria Race Course
June 9/1900

Dear Mother

I have had no time to write before, we have been marching all the time. We left Brandfort on the Tuesday night to march to Kroonstad, 100 miles. We arrived there on the Sunday night. The last day we marched, we started on Saturday night at 5 oclock, went 13 miles had

Fig. 6 Walter and his comrades in khaki in South Africa.
Back row: Hockney, Marris, Beech. Front row: Charlesworth, Rhodes, Barley.

1¹/₂ hours sleep marched another 7, then had breakfast then did the
last 21 arriving at Kroonstad at 8 oclock, 41 miles in 27 hours. I think
that is a record.

Our Regiment was there so we joined them. We are D Company
has their D Co is Mounted Infantry. We had a rest on Monday, on
Tuesday we started to march to the Vaal River, we got there the
following Sunday. We had done 180 miles in eleven days. From there
we went on to Johannesburg, we took it without any opposition. We
marched through the town with fixed bayonets. Lord Roberts was

there and hoisted the old flag. It is a pretty place I should like to live there.

Well from there we went on to Pretoria and arrived within three mile on Whit Monday and we had to fight there. I am very pleased to say none of the Volunteers were hit, but 3 or 4 of the Lincolns were. I wasnt in it, I got lost and found myself among the artillery so instead of being under rifle fire I was under shell fire, my word they do knock things about. I found our camp about ten at night and was very pleased too.

We marched into Pretoria on the Tuesday morning and formed the Guard of Honour for Lord Roberts and his staff. It was all right for them, but we had not anything to eat all day. We are camping on the Race course w[h]ere all our prisoners were confined, about 3 thousand escaped this week and came in to us.

Well we have had some hard times but thank God it is over, has we are going no further. We shall be coming home I expect before you receive this. We have been on half rations and quarter rations, fancy marching 25 miles in one day with nothing else only a biscuit and a bit, you may guess the size of them, 5 to the pound. We have had to make many a meal off a biscuit and a tin of water. We drink any sort of water, dead horses and mules in it or else go without. It is hard lines if you want to buy a biscuit off a fellow, it is from 6d to 2/6, so get prepared when I come home to have something to eat ready.

Tell Kate and Harry I got her letter but not the cigarettes. The heavy marching has knocked me up. I am in Hospital, been in two day, I have a touch of fever. My temperature is 102, but it is nothing to worry about, I only want about a weeks rest to pull me round. I have got a pal here with me from Crowle, I know him well. They call him Kingsley, he is in the 2nd Cold Streams, he knows Union well.

Roll on England I want to be there. I can tell you things better when I get home. Remember me to all

With best love to you and all at Sheffield

Walter

The *Hull Times* published the above letter from Walter to his mother but with most of the family news edited out. In an addendum, the account claimed that, 'Since the letter was written, Barley along with the other Volunteers, was in the battle at Nitral's Nek, but with the rest, emerged unscathed.' This, as can be seen in Walter's letter of 14 July 1900 (Letter 21), was incorrect as Walter, with others of the Volunteers, was unable to march into battle because his boots were worn out.

A news clipping in the Scrapbook in the Museum of Lincolnshire Life gives a rather different view of the Guard of Honour formed by the Volunteers for Lord Roberts. The source and author of the clipping are missing.

A RAGGED REGIMENT

'About 2.30 this afternoon we lined the streets for Lord Roberts passing through and a pretty figure we looked. Our shirts were sticking out of the holes in our coats. My jacket was torn along the back, the back of my trousers out and my knees sticking through the legs. Oh, we were a pretty sight.

'After the march past we camped out on the veld under an old blanket.

'We were roasted during the day and so cold at night you could pick ice off the water in the morning.

'We have two water carts with us on the march and we dare not look at them. The officers use them for a bath and Tommy has to go about two miles if he wants any, so they don't appreciate Tommy much. No-one knows how we get treated. Only them that is out here.'

Private Marris also wrote to his parents about the march to Pretoria. His letter gives more details of incidents on the long march and of the capture of Pretoria that Walter missed when he got lost. He also gives more details of the days after the fall of Pretoria when Walter was in hospital.

Lindsey and Lincolnshire Star, 28 July 1900, p. 5

LETTER FROM THE FRONT

21 June Pretoria

Pte. Marris reported to his parents that he was in the best of health and has had it a bit rough since leaving Brandfort on a convoy to Kroonstadt.

'We had to do some hard marching going nearly all day and night. We arrived at Holfontein on the 20th at 8.30 am, after going 21 miles the previous night and as soon as we got our breakfast we got orders to join our Regiment at Kroonstadt 22 miles away. We set off at 10.30 am and arrived at 7 pm, the men were all done up when we *halted. We were inspected by General Maxwell and Col. Roberts. We moved out of town on Tuesday and had 23 miles march and then went on outpost on a kopje 4 miles off. We did 22 miles next day and came in touch with the enemy but they don't stay. The next place we came in touch with them was Vaal River on Sunday the 27th but they cleared off after our artillery had given them a feather. We crossed the Vaal by wading through over our knees, we marched on three miles to our camp. I got on guard and at some kaffir's house I got the best meal I have had out here. I bought a fowl hot out of the pot and I and a pal had a good meal after being on half rations for a week. We arrived on the hills round Johannesburg on the 30th. We marched round the town at 2.30 pm and got into camp at 5 pm, 2 miles out of the town. It was the first good look I had had of "Bobs", the old man looked well and the people would have given us anything but we were not allowed to receive presents.*

'The next day we marched past the Guards but could not find any of the Scunthorpe chaps. We halted on a kopje 7 miles out of the town. On Whit Monday we were up at 2.45 and marched out in skirmishing order at 5.30, the first time in this order since joining the Regiment. We have had some heavy marching up hill all the time. We saw some cavalry charge a hill on our left front at 12 noon and then we advanced over a kopje and as soon as we got on the ridge we advanced to within hundred yards of the kopje and then bullets began to strike round us so we halted and took cover the best we could behind anthills and bits of stone. We soon begun to have a few shots at the enemy. We advanced to 1,600 and laid down under cover of the stones till 4 pm and kept having a blot at anything we saw move. We advanced again to 1,000 yards and gave them a few more shots. It was a bit thick as we advanced with the bullets flying thickly all round and making the sand fly. We halted for a few minutes and then went for them but they cleared out soon and when we got to their position on the kopje the cavalry was after them at full speed. They did not leave any dead behind them but they must have lost some men as the artillery had done splended work all the time. We could see where the shells had burst.

'We had to march 1$^1/_2$ miles to camp and then got served with half a can of muddy water. It would have given us fever if we had drunk it unboiled. We went to bed without anything. The other company with us had two wounded, we hadn't a hit, although we had some narrow escapes. At six next morning we joined up with the 14th Brigade on our right. Our Regiment was Roberts' Guard of Honour. On prison guard we got ourselves full up with mealy

pudding. The Kaffir police gave us as much as we could take of sugar and mealies. We camped on the race course three days. Then we escorted guns to General French to try and capture Botha. We went 7 miles on trucks and then marched 15 miles till dark and then found Botha had cleared out in the morning. If we had been soon enough we could have captured Botha and all his force but our men gave him something to go on with. The Lancers went through them three times. We next got orders to go and meet Baden-Powell on the Rustenburg Road. We were off in the morning and went 22 miles and then halted for the night and off again at 6 next morning when we met him there was a cheer. He rode up to General Hutton and shook hands and afterwards went through to Pretoria. We got orders to march back in three days. General Hutton went forward and captured 150 Boers, 2 guns and a battery of artillery.

'*I have been on town guard at the Corn Flour Mills. We got boiled mutton and beans for tea at 1s6d. We also got beef sandwiches and tea. We were on half rations from Kroonstadt to Pretoria and had nothing but a pound of flour a day on our last journey and meat when we could get it. Jam was 2s per lb, tinned butter 3s a pound, sugar 9d, Flour 6s a stone but they can sell here at these prices as money is not considered when you are so hungry. We are alright again now.*

There are all sorts of booms in camp about going home. The latest is that we set sail on the 14th July but I think we shall be off before then as our Regiment is all Militia Reserves and Volunteers. All the regulars are down country. When we marched out last Saturday we numbered 95, 20 have dropped out on the march, the rest had bad boots and went sick when ordered on the march. Well I think the war is all but finished now. Methuen has cut De Wet and I don't think Botha is worth going for. The Boers have captured a lot of mails and ours must have been amongst them as there isn't any letter for us and several others have got theirs.

'*Tell Charlie I am alive and kicking but I shan't be able to get any of Kruger's wiskers as he has done a bunk. I have travelled 130 miles and we haven't caught the Boers yet. We are all in tatters and badly shod but we shall get some more from Cape Town.*

From your affectionate son,
Horace Marris 6336 2nd Lincs Regt, Pretoria'

Marris's official name was Walter. Horace must have been a family name.

An item published in the *Hull Times* offers a poignant comment on the sufferings of Boer families in the war. It reports, in a telegram sent from Lorenzo Marques, an interview with the wife of Paul Kruger, the President of the Transvaal. Mrs Kruger had remained in Pretoria after her husband left the city and was never in Lorenzo Marques.

Hull Times, 21 April 1900, p. 8

MRS KRUGER ON THE WAR

A telegram from Lorenzo Marques, dated 13th inst., says:–

Mrs Kruger, in an interview today, said that she trusted God would soon put a stop to the merciless bloodshed, but the Republic would be vigorouly defended even if Pretoria should finally be taken. She said that up to the present time, she had had in the field 33 grandsons, two of whom were killed, four sons, six sons-in-law, and innumerable other relations.

By early July 1900 Walter and his companions were convinced that the war was nearly over and began to look forward to going home. It was obvious, however, from the determination of the Afrikaners to defend the homeland, as expressed by Mrs Kruger, that an early end to the war was unlikely.

Letter 20

July 5/1900
Pretoria

Kiss May for me.

Dear Mother,

We are still at Pretoria. I think we shall stop here while we come home. I have come out of hospital, I was in a fortnight. We are camped about three miles out so it is a long walk there and back to do Town Guard, as we only get one night in bed out of two, what with guards and outpost on the kopjes. We are called out in a morning about four o'clock to stand to arms about four hours until seven o'clock for fear the Boers will attack. We are guarding the west line of hills of the town. We also guard the railway station, the mine and

Bank and Krugers house. I was on guard at Krugers last Sunday, the old lady is there but not him.

I received A Wigfalls cigarettes, thank him for me. I have not got Kates nor shant do has De Wet captured the mails, the dirty blackguard. I shall bring a bit of Kruger money home, pennies are the scarcest. I have seen them sold from 2/6 to 16/- each. I have got two or three. We have a bit of money to draw has we did not get any on the march, we do not get any biscuits because now we get a pound of bread instead, which we eat at one meal. We have to buy some, we pay 6d a loaf, we often eat three a day so you can see what appetites we have. African air agrees with us. We have buried one of the Volunteers and two or three more are not expected to live, our party are all in good health. Alec has had diarhea bad but is better.

We have to be careful with our money has things are dear here, jam 1/6 a pound, butter 3/-, milk 1/6 a tin, matches 2d a box, biscuits 3/- a pound, English Tobacco 8/-, Boer from 1/-, Salmon 1/6, Sardines 1/-, there is nothing here under a Ticky or threepence, they wont sell anything under a ticky without you happen to have coppers and they are scarce now, you have to get sixpennyworth.

There are some splendid buildings here, for instance the bank, Mint, Barracks, Government House and the new Law Courts which cost £3,000,000, it has been turned into a hospital. There is a splendid Museum, there is everything from a mouse to an elephant. There are baths too. The pubs are all closed but we dont seem to care for it now, it is about 2 months since we had any, we think more about eating, we was a fortnight before we got filled up after what we had gone through. Tell Lillie not to insult me any more about mackeral, when we were having dry bread and coffee for tea.

Krugers house or the Presidency has it is called is a common looking low built house, one of the commonest in Pretoria. I think the old hypocrite must be a miser by the look of things. Lillie wanted to know how we spent Whit Monday, it was the day we were fighting outside Pretoria so we shall remember it. Nobody is allowed out in the town after seven at night, if we see anyone and they havent a pass we lock them up. Botha says he will surrender if we give him Pretoria, he gave us 48 hours to clear out or he would attack us, but it hasnt come off yet.

I saw Lockeys letter in the Hull Times. I was pleased to know he was all right. The latest report is that we leave here on the 25th but I expect as usual it is only a rumour but dont write no more after you receive this. I have only received one letter from you in six weeks so perhaps De Wet got them too. Tell Willie Skinner stamps are too dear to buy, 3/6 for six, thank him for writing to me. Remember me to Lizzie and Mr. I have received a letter from Captain Dove, so it shows the letters were saved from the Mexican. Tell Lillie I cant send any flowers, it is winter here and the grass is all dried up, didnt you get the bit of heather I sent her and I have got some boer cartridges and bullets what they have used as relics and a bit of rail.

So goodbye for the present with love to you all.

Walter

Send this to Sheffield, best wishes to J Fowler

From Pte W S Barley, 2nd Lincoln Regiment, Pretoria.

MEANWHILE ...

3 May to 30 June 1900

On 3 May, Lord Roberts with 43,000 troops resumed the march on Pretoria. On the following day a relief column left for Mafeking and relieved the town on 17 May. The Volunteers, who had left Tulbagh with orders to join their regiment, caught up with the 2nd Lincolns at Kroonstad on 20 May and marched with them on Johannesburg. Buller, meanwhile, began his advance from Natal into the Transvaal, in which 'Lockey' took part. His intention was to join up with Roberts near Pretoria.

The Boers retreated north in front of the British advance and continued to disrupt supply lines. On 26 May the British vanguard crossed the Vaal River and a two-pronged attack on Johannesburg began. The city was taken on 31 May but not before the Boer army under Louis Botha had extricated itself and moved north towards Pretoria. This was made possible by a twenty-four-hour armistice granted by Roberts, on condition that the city surrendered peacefully. Roberts still clung to his conviction that the war was nearly over. Walter, with the other Volunteers, marched through Johannesburg and saw the British flag hoisted.

Pretoria was not surrendered so easily. Roberts had, by then, realised that the Johannesburg armistice had allowed Botha, with considerable numbers of men, armaments and other supplies, to take up position near Pretoria. Although many of the Boer leaders now feared that a continuation of the fight was futile, they decided, after another Council of War, that should Pretoria fall, the veld itself must become the battlefield. President Kruger left Pretoria on 27 May on his way into eventual exile in Europe, leaving his wife in the family home. He never saw her again.

On 5 June battle was engaged. Walter described the events even though, by some mischance, he had become separated from his regiment and did not see all the action. Once again Botha managed to gain time for a fighting retreat by offering peace talks over Pretoria. As the Boers fell back the city was taken and a triumphal march-past to honour 'Bobs', in which Walter took part, was hastily arranged. The British prisoners taken in earlier engagements were released from the camp on the racecourse.

The scene was now set for the second phase of the war. In future the Boers, now divided into two armies representing the Orange Free State and the Transvaal, would engage in guerrilla tactics; and the British, in an attempt to deprive them of shelter and supplies, would begin to adopt the controversial 'scorched earth' policy which has, ever since, been held in abhorrence by the Afrikaner people.

De Wet and De la Rey's attacks on British supply lines continued, capturing in one raid, on the railway station at Roodewal, so many military supplies that they were forced to burn much that could not be carried away. This activity was to keep Walter and the Volunteers on guard duty on the hills around Pretoria for the rest of their time in South Africa.

Chapter 6

Disaster at Nitral's Nek

11 July 1900

> *E's only a Tommy – 'e don't count for much*
> *And only 'is mates see him fall.*
> *'E won't 'ave no paragraph all to 'imself*
> *'E done wot they told 'im – that's all.*
>
> *'E done wot they told 'im – wot else could 'e do*
> *'E went out to fight like the rest,*
> *'E done wot they told 'im and England today*
> *Is poorer by one of the best.*
>
> *'E don't leave no widder, no kids as'll care,*
> *It won't break the 'eart of no gal,*
> *Thank Gawd! Then it don't matter much; wot's the odds,*
> *If it just breaks the 'eart of a pal.*
>
> Anon in *Hull Times*, 24 February 1900, p. 4

After the long march to Pretoria and the battles to take both Johannesburg and Pretoria, the Lincolnshire Volunteers were again deployed on what was their main role in the war, guarding areas and installations while the Regular Army engaged in the actual fighting.

The humdrum life of guarding the kopjes came to an abrupt end, at least for a time, on 11 July 1900 when the 2nd Lincolns, supported by the Volunteers, were engaged in what started as a routine holding manoeuvre in the hills to the north of Pretoria where there had been some evidence of Boer activity. The British contingent, made up of one squadron of the Scots Greys, two guns of O Battery of the Royal Horse Artillery and five companies of the Lincolnshire Regiment, were ambushed and, after a full-scale battle, were overcome and the pass at Nitral's Nek was taken by the Boers.

The episode caused great excitement in Lincoln and the surrounding area, and the local press gave it full coverage. The human story of the engagement was told in letters, both published and unpublished, from men involved in the action and its aftermath.

Hull Times, 17 July 1900. The following news items are all from p. 8.

BAD NEWS FOR LINCOLNSHIRE

DISASTER TO THE 2nd LINCOLNS

FIVE COMPANIES SURROUNDED BY BOERS

HEAVY LOSSES AND HEROIC DEEDS NORTH OF PRETORIA

GALLANT FIGHT BY THE TRAPPED COMPANIES

On Friday morning came very bad news for this district. Five companies of the 2nd Lincolns, some Scots Greys, and two guns were surrounded in the mountains north of Pretoria. They resisted with the utmost heroism all day, but in the end were overpowered. The losses were very heavy, most of the Scots Greys being taken prisoner with 90 Lincolns.

The casualty lists will be awaited with foreboding in Hull and North Lincolnshire.

FIVE COMPANIES SURROUNDED

The following despatch, telling of some very unpleasant events in South Africa, was issued by the War Office:–

(From Lord Roberts to the Secretary of State for War)
Pretoria, 12th July, 7.52 p.m.
The enemy having failed in their attempt to get round our right rear, as mentioned in my telegram of the 9th inst., made a determined attack on our right flank yesterday, and I regret to say, succeeded in

capturing Nitral's Nek, garrisoned by one squadron of the Scots Greys, two guns of O Battery of Royal Horse Artillery, and five companies of the Lincolnshire Regiment.

The enemy attacked in superior numbers at dawn and, seizing the hills which commanded the Nek, brought a heavy converging fire upon the small garrison.

Nitral's Nek is about 18 miles from here, near where the road crosses the Crocodile River. It was held by us in order to maintain road and telegraphic communication with Rustenburg.

Fighting lasted more or less throughout the day, and immediately on receiving information in the early morning of the enemy's strength, I despatched reinforcements from here under Colonel Godfrey, King's Royal Scottish Borderers.

Before, however, they reached the spot the garrison was overpowered. The two guns and the greater portion of the squadron of the Greys were captured owing to their horses being shot, as were also about 90 men of the Lincoln Regiment.

GALLANT RESISTANCE OF THE LINCOLNS

PRETORIA, Thursday
Details are to hand of the disaster to the Lincolnshire Regiment.

It appears that five companies were ordered on Wednesday to hold the pass through the Magalesberg in the neighbourhood of Daspoort Fort.

They reached the pass in the afternoon.

Three companies with two guns of O Battery, took up a position in the pass and camped the night there, leaving the other companies in the plain some distance south of the pass.

The eastern hill presented a rugged, rocky and inaccessible face, but further east it was apparently approachable from the main ridge.

At daybreak yesterday, as shots were being fired by the men forming the pickets placed on a small kopje north of the pass, the Boers appeared on the eastern kopje and opened a heavy fire.

Confusion ensued, but the Colonel soon made his voice heard and commanded the men to take up a position on a kopje west of the gap.

Thence a hot fire ensued during the whole day.

Two guns, with an escort of Scots Greys, which had been placed in advance of the main body, were captured, making a heroic resistance.

Nearly every man was killed or wounded.

The Maxim Sergeant brought his gun into action early in the day, but the opposing fire was too hot, and he was obliged to retire.

This he did successfully, saving the gun with the aid of seven Volunteers.

Meanwhile the Boers were keeping up a continuous fire all along the line.

The Lincolns gallantly replied.

About three o'clock the enemy appeared on the left of the British position.

An officer and 15 men made a valiant attempt to charge the enemy.

Fourteen of the little band were killed or wounded.

The three companies of the Lincolns were now practically surrounded but they never wavered.

Their firing was the model of steadiness.

They had to be as economical as possible with their ammunition, as there was no chance of getting further supplies.

Towards nightfall all the ammunition was expended.

The latest arrival from the scene of the engagement states that the men were taking good cover with fixed bayonets at the moment of his escape.

They were awaiting the approach of the enemy.

I have undoubted authority for stating, most positively, that the enemy employed armed natives.

Two leaped from cover when a small party of the Lincolns were surrounded, and demanded the latters' surrender.

A soldier who still had his magazine full, stepped forward and shot both natives dead.

It is feared that the casualties are very heavy.

About thirty men struggled back to camp today.

A great force was assembled to prevent any further progress on the part of the enemy.

The mention of 'armed natives' refers to the general but erroneous belief that the use of 'natives' was outlawed by both sides. Many myths regarding the use of native troops have accumulated but the truth is that both sides used them, mainly as support staff and labourers. Many, however, were armed, as was reluctantly admitted by Kitchener in intelligence reports. Many British soldiers believed that the Boers did not play fair in the use of black soldiers and, therefore, felt entitled to shoot any who were armed, as reported above.[5]

'FORCED TO SURRENDER AT DUSK'
(Times Telegram)

PRETORIA, Thursday, 4.5 [sic] p.m.
An unfortunate occurrence happened yesterday involving the loss of a company of the Lincolns, a squadron of the Scots Greys, and a section of the O Battery.

This force was holding three kopjes at Commando Nek, 18 miles north-west of the town.

Commandant Grobler, at the head of a strong force, with four guns, seized the higher ground to the east early on Wednesday morning, and opened a terrific fire at dawn.

The horses were shot down and the guns rendered useless.

The force held out with the utmost gallantry all day, retiring to the westernmost kopje, where the remants were forced to surrender at dusk.

A force of Norfolk Borderers and an Elswick Battery were despatched at one p.m. but, although they marched hard they could not reach the spot in time.

LINCOLNS' COMMANDING OFFICER WOUNDED AND PRISONER

It is officially reported this afternoon that the casualties at Nitral's Nek include:- Killed: Lieutenant Connolly, Royal Scots; and Second Lieutenant Pilkington, Royal Dragoons.

Colonel Roberts, commanding the Lincolns, was wounded and taken prisoner.

In comparison with the official accounts of the engagement, those of the ordinary soldiers who observed the circumstances of the fight present a different, and more personal, picture.

There follows another news clipping from the Scrapbook in the Museum of Lincolnshire Life. 'From the Special Correspondent with the Lincolns.' No date or source.

NITRAL'S NEK DISASTER
Shoeless, Filthy and Ragged

From Pte A.K. Spence of the Lincs Volunteer Company on active service, who was wounded at Nitral's Nek.

> *'I will give you a little account of it as far as I saw ... We got well started by 6 am on the 10th, the Volunteer Company going down to Daspoort Pass to meet some of the Company coming off town guard. We had to leave about 20 men at Daspoort as they had no boots they could march in. The men were shoeless and in a filthy, ragged condition, but are in good spirits.'*

In the following letter Walter reports the Battle of Nitral's Nek. He was, however, one of those unable to march into battle because their boots had worn out.

Letter 21

Pretoria

July 14th 1900

Dear Mother

Just a few lines to let you know we are all right. As you will have seen that the Lincoln Regiment was cut up. I was not in it again, it seems fated for me not to get in action. They were twenty four of us could not go has our boots were not fit to march in. I think now we were very lucky by the casualties. They went out marching not expecting to fight, about 3 or 4 hundred of them, that was all, and were surprised in a pass, they had no chance as the Boers lined the kopjes, about 2000 of them. We lost in the Volunteers two killed and two wounded, one a Lance Corporal shot through the eye, the other one is from Barton called Hannah. He was shot through the chest but lived two days after, he was as cheerful as anything, wanted a cigarette, he said they have made a rat hole in me. I miss him has he was my bedmate, the fellows say it was awful its a wonder any of them escaped alive.

The report was this morning they had found and buried 85 on one side of the kopje only, so I dont know how many more there will be, if they keep going on there wont be a Lincoln Regiment left. The Regulars say it was worse than Paardeburg and that was a hot spot. One good job is all our fellows are all right, you would feel a bit uneasy I expect while you saw the names mentioned of the killed and wounded. I hear we have got them surrounded so we shall capture them, we heard the heavy guns going last night and today.

Well about other things. We dont know when we are coming home. I expect we shant come while there is any fighting. The latest rumour is we are going to Johannesburg to stop there a while, but on the other hand we heard the Major has volunteered for the front again. He wanted to take us all out again the next day but Lord Roberts said no, the Lincolns have been worked too hard so they can have a rest. We go on outpost every other night from four till five next morning, then from five to seven we patrol the kopjes to see if the boers are about. We have to keep a sharp look out too, has we can see the pass where they were cut up.

We had some clothing sent out, as presents, we received them yesterday. I got two shirts, one handkerchief, 1 muffler and a knitted helmet and got our boots this morning.

Tell Lillie I have sent her a few violets, and a thorn or two, we have to go through those thorns sometimes. Our Captains name is Newsum from Lincoln, timber merchant, he is in hospital. Tell Kate I have given the cigarettes up now, they must have been captured with the mails. I forgot to say only our waggon was saved out of the lot. Our fellows fetched it out under a heavy fire, so we did not lose our blankets nor top coats. I was pleased as all our relics were on, cartridges etc, we have carried them too far to want to lose them. I hope I shall soon get paid else we shant get no Boer money.

A report has just come in that the boers have liberated our prisoners that they captured the other day, has they have no food to feed them on. Well we are tired of it all and wish we were at home to tell you things instead of writing. Tell Trueman I dont think I shall be able to use a Billiard cue, but I will shoot him at the shooting gallery.

We are missing all the good doings you are having but I expect we shall have one too when we get back. I had a letter from our Captain, Capt. Dove, the other day, he said we gave you a good send off but we will give you a better welcome. I hope we all come back safe and sound to enjoy it, because here we think we have a spread fit for a king if we can have dry bread and jam and coffee, cocoa is a big luxury. I have enjoyed many a good meal of sop. I think that is all at present, sent this to Sheffield.

Dear Lillie, I am reckoning of having a week at Sheffield, then you can talk about having mackeral for supper. Love to Kate, Harry, Charlie, kiss the bairns. I expect Ada got my letter.

Give Willie Skinner this stamp and tell him stamps are sold here from 3/6 half a dozen to 5/- each. Remember me to J Fowler and A Wigfall and everybody

With best love Walter

Walter also wrote a letter about the above events to comrades in the Volunteers, dated 4 August 1900. The letter was printed in both the *Lindsey and Lincolnshire Star* and the *Hull Times* on the same day. The addressee is not named.

Lindsey and Lincolnshire Star, 15 September 1900, p. 5
Hull Times, 15 September, p. 7

'We are at Pretoria and have been since June 5th. When we came we formed a guard of honour for Lord Bobs, then camped on the race course and formed the guards for the town. Nobody is allowed out after 7 except by pass. The guards were at the station, Mint, Post Office, Museum, Bank Flour Mills and the Presidency, so we have had the honour of guarding Mrs Kruger. The town is a nice quiet place and has some good buildings. The Government House, new Law Courts are magnificent buildings; then there is the Bank, Mint, PO, Museum, baths etc. Tom Hockney has been promoted to Lance Corporal. Fred Skinner went into hospital and has been sent down country. I was in hospital a fortnight. Charlesworth had dyssentry but is better. The others are allright.

'I suppose you have heard about the Lincolnshires being cut up in the Pass. 24 did not go owing to bad boots. Rhodes, Marris and myself were 3 of the lucky ones. Our Company lost 3 killed and 3 wounded. We have had 2 die of disease, 3 wounded and about 30 in hospital. We had a court martial last week; a volunteer got 56 days of imprisonment for sleeping at his post.

'We have left the race course and are now guarding a range of hills outside. We get 2 nights in bed, 3rd night outpost and have a splendid view of the hills. We can see the Pass clearly where the Lincolnshires were trapped although it is 20 miles away, the air being so clear.

'We are living better now, jam twice a week, rum and bacon once a week. The bacon is a luxury after 6 months bully beef or leather. The marches we did were very trying ones, particularly on short rations; sometimes a biscuit and a quarter to march 25 miles on in a day. I think we did a record march Brandfort to Kroonstad – 42 miles in 24 hours with 1½ hours sleep in it, but that is over for a blessing.

'I think the war is practically over now. We are getting tired of it and hope to be home soon. I had a letter from Capt. Dove. He said we got a good send off but would get a better welcome home. We hope we shall soon come home safe to enjoy it. You have had some good times in England while we have had some hard ones; but I hope it is our *turn next. We have missed 4 holidays. I hope we shan't miss the next one – Christmas – I hear we are going to have a six weeks furlough when we get back, but don't know for a fact. You will be enjoying yourselves today (Bank Holiday) at the Club. I should like a glass of Burton; it is over 3 months since we had any. Please show this to J. Fowler, Sergeant Bugg and the boys at the club as we can't write to all. The boys wish to be remembered to you and all inquiring friends.'*

Although Walter's attention had soon returned to details of day-to-day events and to the hopes of an early return home, the papers continued to provide details of the Nitral's Nek engagement.

Hull Times, 28 August 1900, p. 11

HOW A MAXIM WAS SAVED
BARTON VOLUNTEER AT NITRAL'S NEK

The following is an account of the disaster to the 2nd Lincolns at Nitral's Nek, being extracts from a letter sent by Private Walter Stark, a Barton Volunteer:–

Pretoria, July 22nd
'You will have seen from the papers that we have had another fight, but a very different one to what I had ever seen before. We got caught in a trap and were fighting eight hours. But it was no use – they were too many for us, and got on our flanks. We then got orders to try to get away, as we had lost the greater part of our regiment. Only a few of us went.'

'There was only me and George Hannah there from Barton, and he got a bullet through his chest. The other Volunteers stayed at Pretoria with bad boots. I will always remember that day as long as I live.'

Stark saw a Lance-Corporal carried away. 'He had got shot right through the head and died after a few minutes.' He then saw George Hannah carried past on a stretcher. 'I saw it was my only comrade from Barton ... as he passed he saw me.'

'I felt very queer for a few minutes, but it soon wore off, and I forgot everything but fighting. I stuck to it until we got orders to retire, and then eight of our Volunteers pulled a Maxim gun through

the thick of the firing. It was a mystery how we got out with it. I can tell you the bullets were dropping like rain amongst us, but we got clear and safe.'

Much was made in the papers of the rescue of the Maxim gun.

Hull Times, 21 July 1900, p. 8

GALLANT SERGEANT RAWDIN OF THE LINCOLNS

In describing the affair at Nitral's Nek, a correspondent speaks of 'the most heroic thing in the Lincolns' fight' as being 'the conduct of Sergeant Rawson in working a Maxim gun'.

The Rector of Bottesford, Notts, writes to say that the sergeant's correct name is Rawdin, and that he was born and bred in the village of Bottesford.

The heroism of Sergeant Rawdin is also mentioned in the second of the following reports of the return of many of those taken prisoner in the engagement. Walter reported the 'escape' in Letter 21 but claimed that the prisoners had been released by the Boers as they did not have food for them. The Boers frequently released prisoners as they would have handicapped them in their strategy of guerilla warfare.

A report in the *Hull Times*, on the same day as the news of Nitral's Nek, referred to this Boer practice. The captives, who should not be confused with those taken at Nitral's Nek, were released to fend for themselves until they could rejoin their regiments. It was not uncommon for captured British soldiers to be relieved of their uniforms by the Boers. This may have been due to their desperate shortage of clothing but, no doubt, the uniforms also had value to them as camouflage. Kipling's Piet, in the poem of that name, is described as 'dressed in stolen uniform with badge o' rank complete'.[6]

Hull Times, 14 July 1900, p. 8

800 BRITISH PRISONERS RELEASED

Indignation is generally expressed at the treatment to which the prisoners taken by De Wet and put over the Natal border recently were subjected. The 800 Yeomanry and Militia who were released were in a starving condition. They had been robbed of their khaki uniforms, and been compelled to put on the filthy clothes discarded by the Boers.

This is abominable. It should at once be clearly intimated to the Boers that by treating our men thus barbarously they will in future only be acting directly against the interests of their men who are in our hands.

Hull Times, 21 July 1900, p. 8

CAPTURED LINCOLNS ESCAPE
ECHOES OF THE DISASTER
(Daily Telegraph *Correspondent*)

PRETORIA Sunday 4.30 p.m.
Most of the Lincolns captured at Mosilikzes (sic. Mosilikatze or Mzilikazi) Nek have escaped. Wounded officers with their kits are being sent in by the Boers, but the enemy have declined as a rule the services of our surgeons for their wounded. They admit having sustained considerable losses.

The Scots Greys who had been taken prisoners are also escaping.

The most heroic thing in the Lincolns' fight was the conduct of Sergeant Rawson, who worked the Maxim which was supporting the D and F Companies.

The enemy concentrating a venomous fire upon the Maxim, he ordered the others to retire, and remained alone serving the gun. The Maxim actually jammed under fire. He then dissected it.

Recoupling the parts he resumed firing the gun, which was saved from capture by Volunteers of the D Company, who dragged it out. The weapon is pitted with bullet marks.

Later in the same report, the wounding of George Hannah was recalled.

In the first list of Nitral's Nek casualties issued from the War Office on Monday, appears the name of Private George Hannah. This is the name of a Barton Volunteer, a young man who lived with his parents at the Maltkiln, and was employed by the Farmers Company. There is little doubt they are the same, as the regimental numbers correspond.

The implications of this report, and of the mention of him by Walter in Letter 21, are that Hannah had been mortally wounded. The following letter proves, however, that this was not so.

Hull Times, 22 September 1900, p. 7

LETTER FROM PRIVATE HANNAH OF BARTON

On Sunday a letter was received from Private Hannah, the Barton Volunteer, who was wounded at Nitral's Nek. The letter was received by Mrs Robinson, Green-lane, and is the first written by Hannah since his mishap:–

Imp. Yeomanry Hospital, Dielfontein, August 27th
'I am very sorry to tell you I was shot through the chest on the right side. The affair happened 18 miles west of Pretoria. I was taken to the Volks Hospital and was there a fortnight. When the doctor thought me fit for moving, I was put in the ambulance train for England. I was on the train a week, and was taken bad, and put out here on Bank Holiday.

'We have good attendance here, and live well. I have two eggs and bread for breakfast, pudding, tinned chicken, and a small bottle of stout for dinner, bread and jam for tea. I should have written before, but I was not able to sit up in bed until a few days ago. I left all the Barton boys in good health and spirits.

'I expect to be home the end of October'

MEANWHILE ...

The Ambush at Nitral's Nek – 11 July 1900

The disaster at Nitral's Nek at the hands of General Koos De la Rey and Commandant Grobler, which befell the force of which the 2nd Lincolns were a part, was one of the warnings to the British of the effective guerrilla tactics being employed by the Boers. They were succeeding, at last, in denting – but not fully dispelling – Roberts's confidence that the war was almost over.

Walter's assertion that the war had only several weeks to run was not borne out by the facts. Far from being 'rounded up', as he claimed, De la Rey was able to slip away from the engagement taking British prisoners with him. They were not held for long, however, as the reality of guerrilla warfare was the need to keep moving without the encumbrance of prisoners.

Despite several local successes, the Boers were about to suffer several serious setbacks that would cause their leaders, in October, to gather at a remote farmstead to re-evaluate their military position and strategy.

Chapter 7

Guarding the Kopjes

July to October 1900

> *Only two African kopjes,*
> *Only the cart-tracks that wind*
> *Empty and open between 'em,*
> *Only the Transvaal behind;*
> *Only an Aldershot column*
> *Marching to conquer the land ...*
> *Only a sudden and solemn*
> *Visit, unarmed, to the Rand.*
>
> *Then scorn not the African kopje,*
> *The kopje that smiles in the heat,*
> *The wholly unoccupied kopje,*
> *The home of Cornelius and Piet.*
> *You can never be sure of your kopje,*
> *But of this be you blooming well sure,*
> *A kopje is always a kopje,*
> *And a Boojer is always a Boer!*

Kipling – 'Two Kopjes (Lesson for Yeomanry)'

After the disaster at Nitral's Nek the task of guarding the hills around Pretoria took on a more serious note since ambush was a constant threat. As the following letter shows, the task for the Volunteers was largely routine but, after Nitral's Nek, extreme vigilance was necessary.

Letter 22

Salt some kidney beans

Pretoria

Aug 5th 1900

Dear Mother

We are still at Pretoria and expect to stop here while we come home. We still keep on the range of hills which we are guarding, we are improving now we get two nights in bed and one out. It is Sunday afternoon and me, Rhodes and Marris and a corporal are on top of the hill on observation duty, keeping a look out. We have just had a narrow escape, we had just finished boiling some coffee and had left the fire when a cartridge exploded in the fire, blowing the fire for yards. Has luck would have it the bullet struck downwards but we might have been blinded for life. We have a splendid view up here, the air is so clear we have seen the boers on the opposite side of the valley on another range of hills, four miles distant, it only looks half a mile.

The war is practically over, the net is gradually drawing in, we give it another fortnight as the boers are thoroughly demoralized. We are starting to live a bit better now, we get jam $^1/_4$lb each every two days, rum once a week about 2d worth and bacon once a week $^1/_4$lb, that is a luxury after boiled beef for six months.

You will have to excuse me not writing. We have not had any money for a month, we got £2 on Friday but it soon goes here, things are so dear. Hockney has been promoted to Lance Corporal, Skinner went into hospital and has been sent down country so will soon be home I expect. I have seen Jack Bells brother, him that stayed at our house, he is coming to see you when he gets back, if he gets back. I havent seen him since the Lincolns were surprised by the boers. I have also seen Johnson, him that was groom to Dr Couldreys, he is also in the Lincolns. I got a Hull Times and saw Lockeys photo [Fig. 7] but there is no resemblance.

I want to bring some Kruger money home if we get paid before we leave Pretoria has it is fetching a bit of money in England. We have £3 more to come so you see we have had to save money out of 1/3 per day. It is above three months since we had any beer so I think we are teatootlers now. We are better without it here, as it heats the blood. Horncastle men are not doing very well, there are four of them, one died, one bad in hospital, one 28 days fatigue and one 56 days imprisonment for sleeping at their posts while on outpost. It makes you sleepy not getting plenty of bed and it is as silent as the grave on

Fig. 7 Line drawing of Arthur Lockwood, published in the *Hull Times* (23 June 1900).

the hills. We have two hours work every morning building walls and making roads from one outpost to another.

I enclose a flower or two for Lilly. I got them from a boer farm house. Give Willie Skinner these stamps and the one on the envelope. I do miss my Woodbines. Tell Lillie I am reckoning on my week at Sheffield so get a bed well aired.

I heard we were going to have a six weeks furlough when we come home instead of being dismissed at once, so that will be a holiday for us and get 12/3 a week for it.

Remember me to J Fowler, he will be at camp now. We cant get any Kruger pennies now, they have stopped issuing them, so they will fetch a bit in England. Kiss May for me, tell Ada uncle will soon come home. Send this to Sheffield, remember me to A Wigfall. I am going to miss all vegetables.

With love to all
Walter

The following letter from Sergeant Hancock, a Volunteer of the East Yorkshire Regiment which travelled out on the *Guelph* with the Lincolnshire Volunteers, was published in the 'War By Letter' series of the *Hull Times*. It gives a detailed picture of the role of the Volunteers and the conditions under which they served. While the Lincolns were engaged in the Transvaal guarding the hills around Pretoria, the East Yorks were to the south in the Orange Free State on guard duty in the Biddulphsberg mountains, near the border of Basutoland, now Lesotho. The parentheses in the letter are Hancock's own.

Hull Times, 15 September 1900, p. 11

Biddulphsberg
'*On Friday (20th July) the right half company was kept busy strengthening trenches, and constructing new ones, also in pacing distance, marking the ranges by erecting small trees that had been cut down from the mountain sides.*

'*During the afternoon I climbed to the top of the peak of the mountain, a thousand feet above the Observation Post (6,500 feet above the level of the sea.) From this position there is a fine view of the country.*

'*The Drakensberg Mountains look very pretty in the distant background, with their cloak of snow, making a pleasant contrast against the black kops and kopjes in front of them, and the less distant valleys, some parts burnt black and others covered with khaki coloured grass and soil.*

'On Saturday morning, shortly after five o'clock, No.1 Section had marched to the trenches about half a mile from camp, to support No. 2 Section which had been on outpost during the night. All was quiet, and the morning was exceptionally dark, when suddenly a rifle shot was heard to our right. The bullet whizzed past us and struck the peak with a "ping" quite close to No. 2 Section. We could not find out who fired the shot, but there was no further firing.

'On Saturday night it was the Volunteer Company's turn to furnish all regimental duties. I took twelve men of No. 4 Section on detached post to a ruined Kaffir location on the plain about half-a-mile to the east in the direction of the road to Bethlehem, with orders in case of attack to retire and support a 15-pounder gun. Nothing unusual occurred, and we returned to camp at breakfast time. No. 3 Section was on outpost, having relieved No. 2 Section. The right half company had its turn in camp. On Sunday morning we were very hard at work building sangars. About 6.30 p.m. rain began to fall and by 7 it came down in torrents, the wind blowing a perfect hurricane, bringing tents down and squandering piles of rifles in all directions. Many of the tents that stood the wind were flooded by the rain. It was a happy night, especially for men on guard and outpost duties. Tuesday (23rd July) being a lovely bright day, we had a pleasant 24 hours of duty.

'At night a strong wind began to blow, accompanied by a slight rainfall. Next morning the wind had become so strong that we couldn't get our fires to burn, so we could not do any cooking. The men mostly contented themselves by sitting in their tents (we have five tents per company of over one hundred men) and singing, with our raw meat "staring us in the face".

'We had a special treat on this eventful day, in the form of a quarter pound of jam per man. Didn't we have a royal time of it. We shall never want to leave South Africa again if they squandered such luxuries amongst us in such generous quantities. Somebody mentioned "A bit of good bread and butter". We begin to wonder what it's like. We understand the meaning of "B. and B." (bully and biscuit) but we never see any of the former now. We have to make all our dainty dishes out of biscuits (patent dog biscuits). We only get, on the average, about four a day, so we dare not make them too nice, or we should eat a day's ration at one meal, but when we can get a couple of

biscuits in hand, we can, by a stretch of imagination, make a nice tin of gruel by smashing them very small and boiling them in water, or we can even make porridge by thickening with more biscuit.

'Then again a nice suet pudding is made from these obliging biscuits by boiling them in water, then putting them in the "inner ration" of half a pint of "mutton bone soup" into which the shadow of a square of compressed vegetables has been mixed. Of course we can't expect them to actually put the vegetables in the soup; it might overload our stomachs, then we could not possibly be able to build sangars or "go navvying" (digging trenches), and we might possibly get indigestion and fall asleep on "Sentry Go", which offence makes a soldier on active service liable to the penalty of death.

'On Thursday afternoon I kept up the half-holiday by taking my rifle and taking a walk round the base of the peak of Biddulphsberg. On reaching the Western side we found the Boer trenches from which the Guards met their disaster, with the black veldt in front where they were burned.

'On Friday morning a large convoy was seen crossing the veldt from the direction of Senekal. A party was sent out from our regiment to see if they had any letter bags for the East Yorks. My section was for outpost so we had to march away without knowing the latest from the base, but even in the most advanced trenches the "Good News" reached us by eight o'clock.

'"There's some letters for us!"

'Then faces brighten; somebody ventures the remark, "I wonder if there's a letter for me", another remarks, "Will my promised tobacco turn up?" Another chap chimes in rather sadly, "I've had no news from home yet. I do hope there's something for me", and so passes the night, the event giving one plenty of food for reflection while doing the weary patrols and sentry-go's, watching over the dreary plains.

'The men in camp received their welcome missives the same night, and it goes without saying that detached duties send in for their "News from Home" as soon as day breaks; the letters are given out, up comes the coffee about the same time, and it is really surprising what a nice breakfast one can make on biscuit and letters, although a few find the repast less palatable, who have been "forgotten".

'Saturday night promised to be a quiet night in tents for No.1 Section, with a quiet day of rest to follow, but alas, by 7 p.m. the signallers were very busy and soon it was apparent that a move was

to be made. Shortly afterwards "Orderly Sergeants" were called for (no bugles are sounded here), and we were soon made aware of what was in store for us. G Company was to go to Senekal to join the other half battalion. E, H, and Volunteer Company were to go to Hammonia (about 35 miles).

'On Sunday morning "arouse" at 4 a.m.; before six all tents were struck and packed (along with baggage) on the waggons. We sat down (on the ground) for breakfast in complete darkness, and finished it in broad daylight (daylight is very quick here). We were soon ready to "fall in". Stores and ammunition were then packed, and at eight all was ready for marching off, but an unexpected treat was awaiting us.

'A small party had brought more letters; they were soon given out by Companies, and I was soon knelt in front of the company with a heap of letters on the ground, calling out the names that eager ears were listening for.

'Even this pleasant duty had its solemn parts, for a little heap kept swelling with a number of unclaimed messages, which are dropped with such remarks as, "He's invalided", "He's sick in hospital", and occasionally the more regrettable remark, "He's gone".

'The Fourth Commandment of the East Yorkshire Regiment seems to be "Six days shalt thou labour, and do overtime on the seventh".

'All hands were roused on Monday morning at 2 a.m., waggons packed and began to file off at 3; the Volunteer Company which formed the rearguard followed a quarter of an hour later, arriving at Klip Drift Nek at 7.45, having marched 10 miles without breakfast. At this place coffee was served out, and there was a rest of four hours for man and beast. Ten miles later we outspanned at Hammonia, about 5 p.m., the distance travelled in the two days being about 35 miles. Tea was dished out, also raw meat and biscuits. Then we began to "stow away" our second meal of the day. While we were halted at Klip Drift, a message was received by heliograph to the effect that Prinsloo had offered to surrender with 5,000 rebels, with all their waggons and guns.

'It was the same old tale; just as we were getting near, to have a "pop" at them, they must either retire "pellmell" or surrender. One might be excused for thinking they were afraid of trying the mettle of the Volunteer Company; but all joking apart, the plan of Lord Roberts seems all to have been excellent.

'On Tuesday morning we did not "stand to arms". It was daylight when we were roused. E Company moved away at 9 a.m. to take up a position at Commando Nek; the Volunteer Company and H Company stopping to garrison Hammonia.

'By noon a few farmers had come in with their waggons to sell provisions. The general prices of the few things they brought were; Mealy bread, 9d per pound; dried fruits, 1s 6d per pound; chicken (roasted), 2s; turkeys, 11s; hams, 10s (about 8 lbs); eggs, 2s per dozen. Of course, although Mr. Atkins had been hungry and badly fed for some time, he could not afford any more than bread, with very few exceptions.

'The officers had a good time. We had the glorious advantage of seeing these cooked dainties as they were handed out of the carts. Had these been hot we might have got a waft of their savoury smells, but, sad to say, they were all cold.

'It is now Wednesday, the 1st of August. A detachment of Manchesters, (who have been here some weeks) are going to Flicksberg, so they are taking our letters with them, from which place they will probably be sent across the Basutoland border to Durban for shipment to England.

'The health of the Volunteers is remarkably good, considering the great change they have made in their mode of life.

'The change between the living of a fairly well-to-do civilian and a soldier with the Field Force is great indeed!

(7000) SERGEANT W. HANCOCK'

The disaster to the Guards at Biddulphsberg, mentioned by Sergeant Hancock, took place on 29 May 1900. Lieutenant-General Sir Leslie Rundle launched an attack on J.H. de Villiers at Biddulphsberg. Among the British troops were a company each of the 2nd Grenadier Guards and the 2nd Scots Guards. The 2nd Grenadiers were caught in a veld fire, started accidentally, which came upon them from the rear and was carried through their ranks by the wind. The British withdrew.[7]

Letter 23

Pretoria

Aug 6th 1900

Dear Lillie

Just a few lines to let you know things are all right with us. I am writing to Mother at the same time so you will get the letter and see all the news. I have a bit of time on my hands this afternoon so thought I would drop a line to pass time away. If I had been in England I should have been at camp. We never expected being away so long, so I shant get any vegetables out of the garden except spuds, so I shall get home in time for the work of digging them. I have told Mother to salt some for me. I expect you will be gadding about today being Bank Holiday and here we are missing everything. I got Kates cigarettes yesterday so am having a good smoke for we only buy Boer bacca here, about 1/6 a pound, a 3d packet of cigarettes cost 1/- so we dont buy any.

I got to know why G Fidell left Stamps for here in Africa, it was for taking things home. Stamp caught him with a piece of bacon wrapt in his apron under his arm going to breakfast so it was no wonder they could live and the girl he was courting sacked him and she had a bit of money too so he made a bad spec of it.

We are hoping to be out of Africa the end of August, we reckon we shall be home by Hull Fair. I hope so, we are about tired of it. I am in good health since I came out of hospital, my temperature did not go any higher than 102. I have got a little bit of Rheumatic in my bad leg through always sleeping on the ground.

We have a splendid view of Pretoria w[h]ere we are camped on the hills. Pretoria is in the valley. If any of our fellows had brought a camera he could have made some money in England out of it. I hope we get paid before we leave here so as I can bring some Kruger money home. I expect it will go like ripe cherries in England. I expect you and Kate will want something to make a brooch with.

I should like to meet Lockey in Pretoria, he is with Buller not far from here, they will get here in time. We can go into town nearly any time we like, if we ask for a pass. We have been without money for a month now but got paid £2 on account on Friday which leaves them owing me £3-2-6 up to today. If I get that I shall bring some Kruger back.

Our main food is mealie (ground Indian corn) which we make like gruel, we eat stones of it to fill us up because one pound of bread is no

use here. I have eaten three one pound loaves in a day. We spend all
our money in eating, there is no drink to be got. I went out on
Saturday to get something to eat and this is what it cost, just one visit.

4lb mealie	1–0
1lb sugar at 6d	6
1lb sugar at 1/-	1–0
tobacco	1–0
Salts	8
Box of matches	3
2 penny packets of egg powder 3d each	6
1lb rice	1–0
stamps	6
candles 2	6
	6–6

So you see money goes here. Tell Ada a gentleman is sending a big
ship to bring uncle in. I sent some flowers in Mothers letter. I did not
tell Mother about Fidell has she lets Mr Fowler read it, so tell her.
Dont write no more.

Love to all   Walter

Walter mentions his friend Trooper Arthur Lockwood in several letters, but there
is no evidence that they ever met in South Africa. Letters to local papers from
'Lockey', as Walter called him, were published on at least two occasions. The following letter tells of an engagement with the Boers as the 19th Hussars moved into
the Transvaal from Natal. The letter does not state when the engagement
described took place. It was probably after the Battle of Belfast (Bergendal) on 27
August, as Botha and his commando fled north.

Lindsey and Lincolnshire Star, 22 December 1900, p. 5

A LOCAL RESERVIST AT THE FRONT
A MOONLIGHT CHARGE

*Lydenburg, 18 November – Trooper A. Lockwood, 19th Hussars, of
Scunthorpe, writing to his parents:–*
    *'You will have seen in the papers about our moonlight charge into
the Boers near here. It was at 2 a.m. and we were going to attack*

them at daybreak. We were going about so quietly, when all at once they gave it us hot. They had got the clue and were waiting for us. We had to gallop for it and ran straight into another lot of the enemy right in front. They gave it us left and right. They were only 150 yards from us but could not hit us … Two sentries of the Boers challenged our men but we all shouted "Charge", and the sentries ran for their horses, but two of our men caught them and put the sword straight through them. Then we all charged the lot. There were 150 of them and only 70 of us. They went for their lives and we after them. It was bad ground, very rocky and we kept falling. We cut then down as fast as we could catch them. A lot got away as they had better horses. We galloped them five miles. When we got through them we called the roll and there were 13 of us missing; one shot in the head, since dead. All the others turned up next day. One fellow had his leg broken and had ridden 15 miles like that.'

Letter 24

Pretoria
Aug 23rd 1900

Dear Mother

We are still at Pretoria and waiting anxiously for the order to come home, it will not be long if they can only capture Botha or De Wet, if one is caught the others will give in. De Wet has only 500 men now which he managed to escape with. He is a clever general but lucky, always managing to escape if nearly surrounded, but I think his innings is nearly at an end now has there is a column after him.

I saw two of the 19th Hussars in town the other day. I asked them if they knew Locky, they did so I told them to tell him Barley was at Pretoria. They are only about 30 miles out so I shall be able to see him soon. He has not been in any engagement so he is lucky too. Tell Trueman I have had a game at Billiards in Pretoria and won easy, but could not play as well as I do at home, it was at the soldiers home, a full sized board. It is a nice place to go, a large concert room, a large reading and writing room, billiards etc. You can get a cup of tea and a bun for threepence, or lemonade and ginger beer for two pence, cheap isnt it, I had a buster.

I suppose you will have heard about poor Skinner, died from enteric at Bloemfontein, he died 5 days after he left us. His poor mother will be in a way has he was the favourite at home. We were all

93

talking about the good time we should have when we got home and him to go like that, one of the strongest of the party, but man proposes and God disposes. He was never the same after that fight, it seemed to cut him up somehow. Well lets hope the rest comes home safe.

I see in the Hull Times you got the cablegram, we thought it would relieve you all. Our new clothes has come up and boots so we look more respectable now. The other draft of Volunteers came up yesterday and are now with us.

You will get to know before us when we are coming home, you will see it in the papers. You know more about the war than we do. We are out on Observation Hill today, me, Teddy Cross from Brigg and a Horncastle fellow. I am just watching a big convoy come in, it is about seven mile long, they have got about a 100 prisoners with them.

We went out on Monday about 8 mile to scour a wood, supposed to be some boers in, who had been setting fire to the veldt, but did not find any. We captured about 20 niggers, 1 hare, 2 pigeons, 1 horse some cattle and donkeys. Our Captain has come back again, he is better. We heard it was in the papers in England that us and the Yeomanry were going to [de]mobolise the 11th of September, but you will know better than us. I hope it is true.

Remember me to J Fowler and ask him how camp went down this year. Remember me to A Wigfall. Tell him I have got the little knife safe yet, and remember me to everyone.

Love to all at Sheffield, hoping you are all well has I am all right.

With best love to you
Walter

Have you got kidney beans salted yet

Lindsey and Lincolnshire Star, 18 August 1900

DEATH OF A VOLUNTEER

Pte F. Skinner died at Bloemfontein of enteric fever on 12 July. He was one of the smartest men sent out from this district.

A Memorial Service has been held for Private Fred Skinner with the Volunteers and Captains Dove and Clifford present.

The following letter from Private T. Tidswell, Militia Reserve, was published in the *Lindsey and Lincolnshire Star*. An earlier letter in the *Hull Times* on 17 March 1900 had shown that he had been at the relief of Ladysmith. He had been in hospital with enteric fever.

***Lindsey and Lincolnshire Star*, 1 September 1900, p. 5**

> *'What do Lincolnshire people think of their men now, both regulars and volunteers? They will fight or die in the attempt. We hope to be home before Christmas. Both officers and men have had enough of it, especially the infantry as it is nothing but march, march from morning till night.'*

MEANWHILE ...

Mid-July to 25 October 1900

The month of July saw the Orange Free State armies of De Wet and President Steyn concentrated in the Brandwater Basin in the mountains to the north of the border of Basutoland, now Lesotho. Major-General Sir Archibald Hunter, with 2,000 men, was sent to cut them off by closing the passes, but this he failed to do in time to prevent Steyn and De Wet slipping away on the night of 15 July over Slabberts Nek, the most central of the six passes. The passes were then taken and closed one by one until, with the closure of Slabberts Nek on 23 July, the trap was finally set. Marthinus Prinsloo, with over four thousand Free Staters, surrendered and was taken prisoner. These were the events commented on by Sergeant Hancock of the East Yorks Volunteers who were guarding the lines of communication to the west of the mountains.

Attention then turned to the pursuit of De Wet, who had retreated north. He was more determined than ever to continue the fight and crossed the Vaal on 6 August by the only drift left unguarded. Despite being closely followed, De Wet succeeded in escaping through Olifants Nek in the Magaliesberg to the west of the Rand.

Having lost a major opportunity of bringing the war to a speedy end, Lord Roberts now turned his attention to capturing Botha, who, with the Transvaal commando, was to the north-west of the Rand. Buller, meanwhile, had completed his sweep from Natal and joined up with Roberts on 20 August. He had succeeded in clearing the Natal railway, thus linking it with Pretoria and transforming Roberts's supply situation. The two armies were now poised for a combined assault on Botha. It was Buller who, on 27 August at the Battle of Belfast, assessed the key to Botha's position as the kopje in the centre of the twenty-mile front. The capture of this salient caused the collapse of both Boer flanks, and Botha fled to the north. Two thousand British prisoners were released at Nooigedacht as the pursuit of Botha continued. Buller captured Lydenburg on 6 September.

It was now the time for departures. President Kruger left his native land on 19 October and sailed into exile. On 24 October, Buller sailed for England to a hero's welcome by the people but official disdain. Lord Roberts was not far behind. He left South Africa in December after handing over to Lord Kitchener as Commander-in-Chief.

Chapter 8

'Almost Over': Waiting for Demobilisation

September to December 1900

We've rode and fought and ate and drunk as rations come to hand,
Together for a year or more around this stinkin' land:
Now you are going home again, but we must see it through.
We needn't tell we liked you well. Good-bye – good luck to you!

Kipling – 'The Parting of the Columns'

After the excitement of the long march into the Transvaal, the battles for Johannesburg and Pretoria, and the débâcle at Nitral's Nek, the Volunteers settled down to their guard duties on the Daspoort Range. Although it was not clear from their terms of service how long they would have to remain in South Africa, rumours about their imminent repatriation abounded; but the weeks went by without any firm news of demobilisation.

Letter 25

Pretoria
Sept 6th 1900

Dear Mother
    Just a few lines to let you know things are all right. We are only getting one night in bed in two has the other company has left us to take charge of a fort. We are patiently waiting for home, we hear that

50,000 are going to be sent home next month so we are hoping to be included with them. We have been served out with new clothes, boots, shoes and socks, but I have only one shirt, there was not enough to go round, so we drew lots for them. They have also given us another writing wallet, 24 envelopes, 24 sheets of paper and a pencil. We got a pay this week £3 so we are not short of money.

My ears are getting bad again. I have had them syringed. The Captain caught me on outpost last night by surprise, he got up to me without me hearing him. He asked me if I was deaf. I told him yes, so he told me to see him this morning, so perhaps I shall get off outpost.

We have just had rum served out and I have bought another ration for six pence so I am having a nice drink while I am writing this. The Horncastle fellow that was dead took us by surprise by marching into camp the other day. I wish poor Skinner would do the same.

It is not often that we get three winters in one year, but we shall. We had winter at Lincoln, winter here and coming home for another. You will have heard that the boers have liberated all our prisoners except the officers, the Lincoln prisoners that were captured in that fight, that is all the reserve men, are coming home. I am pleased that they are keeping our Colonel, Colonel Roberts, to give him a taste of hunger same has we have had, for when we were on the march he would use two or three buckets of good water to bath himself with, and us dying for a drink and not having a wash for perhaps a week. He is a fine built fellow over six feet, but now the prisoners say he is like two lathes, he has had to live like the privates on mealie pap.

Some fool had wrote in the paper that they were harder worked at camp than we were here. I think he must be daft, he wants to come out here and then write from experience. He wants to have our outpost 4 nights up one week 3 nights next and fatigue work in the daytime. I have nothing else to say has it is the same hum drum life every day.

Love to all at Sheffield. Remember me to all,

With best love
Walter

Captains ordered me to go sick with my ears. I havent seen Doctor yet, but I expect to get off outpost.

Letter 26

Pretoria
Sept 13th 1900

Dear Mother

Just another few lines to say things are all right. I went to the doctor with my ears, had them syringed again but it has not done them any good, but I have got off outpost and are ration carrier instead, taking breakfast and dinner up the mountain for the observation party, so I get plenty of bed now. We are living well now, we get bacon, cheese, rum, jam and lime juice, two or three times a week.

Alec told me about Frank Johnson dying and Maria getting married the day after, a bit thick that. We have had another fellow died in hospital, Goodhand from Spelsby so we are losing a few. Alec has been bad with dysentry this last few days but is coming all right again.

We hear we are going to [de]mobolize next month but we hear so many burns. I dont care how soon, else we shall get our year in. Captain says he thinks we shall eat our Christmas dinner in England. I think so too, with a drop of good beer to it, nearly five months teetootal now.

We are sleeping in tents now and have plenty of clothes, money and food so we have nothing to grumble at, only it is not England. Alec says they have sent us some more tobacco out but we have not got it yet. I hope it soon comes to have a bit of English. Things are still dear, but we have got some matches yesterday $1^1/_2$d a box, that is cheap after paying 3d.

Give these stamps to Willie Skinner. I think that is all I have to tell you, things is quiet here now, the same life every day. Remember me to all, love to all at Sheffield.

Walter

I see in the paper they had a tremendous storm at camp, it sounded like the storms we get out here.

So long for the present

Letter 27

Pretoria
Sept 27th

Dear Mother

Still alive, Alec has come out of hospital. Hockney has gone down country very bad, it will not surprise me if he pegs out, but you need not mention it.

I went to town last Tuesday and thought I would have a good blow out has I had won a bit at cards, paid 4/- for dinner, a good spread, 5/- for a pint bottle of Allsopps beer which went down very well. I bought two threepenny pieces for 4/-, so you see we can easy spend money.

Any of us can get our discharge at once if we have a job to go to. Several have gone but I shall come home with the Company, it is too hot up here for painters, for me anyhow. C.I.V. goes on Monday, I expect we shall follow them the middle of the month. Dinner just ready, have got to go up the hills so I have no more time to write, as the mail goes at dinnertime.

With love to all at Sheffield
best love
Walter

Save some kidney beans. Kiss May for uncle

Letter 28

Oct 3/1900
Daspoort Range, Pretoria

Dear Mother

I received your letter last week, you had to write then through us being so long coming home. I got one of Kates letters she sent last May, so I have sent the envelope just as I received it, it will do for a curiosity. We have been told the Volunteers, Yeomanry and reserve men Section D are next on the list for home, I hope so.

We are expecting Lord Roberts to proclaim peace on the 11th or 12th of this month because it will be a twelvemonth since the war started and no nation can declare war against England for three year, after a war has lasted a year. The war is practically over now has hundreds of the burghers are coming in and surrendering. Erasmus surrendered yesterday so it is only a matter of a few days. Botha is going round and advising them to chuck it, they dont even know that Pretoria is in the hands of the British. I saw about 100 of them in the town last Monday that had come in to surrender.

Stores is starting to come into the town now and are going to be cheaper. I had another good feed in Town and finished up with three whiskies, 1/- each and a 1/- worth of strawberries, then bought a dozen eggs 4/-, to take into camp to eat to our bacon.

I have wrote to J Fowler and C.A. Cheesman. I see Tom Beech gets no letter, has he the cheek to stop in the company. We have not heard how Hockney is since he went down country. I still keep my job, ration carrying up the randjes but I get every night in bed and no fatigues to do, so that is all right.

We have been told that we should get no more pay in Africa so that means coming home this month. Have you been getting my letters regularly, because I have been writing every week since we got settled down here. I have got three letters from you since we have been here, that is three months but perhaps you did not write through me telling you not to. So dont write no more because it will be seven or eight weeks before it arrives here, and we expect to be near England then.

Remember me to everybody. Love to all at Sheffield. Tell Ada that a big ship has got ready to bring uncle home.

Kiss May for me

With best love
Walter

Letter 29

Daspoort Range
Oct 18th 1900
Pretoria
Dear Mother

We are still here waiting anxiously for the order to move. Our Captain has sent an application for us to guard prisoners down to the Cape. I hope he succeeds. We cant be long now has several companies of Volunteers has gone down, and it is an order that those men in hospital have to join B Company if not better before we leave. We are under a minutes notice to get ready but it is sickening the suspense of waiting, if we knew the day we could manage all right.

We have had two letters from Hockney, he has been in the convent hospital at Bloemfontein but has been sent to the Cape to be invalided home as he is only recovering very slowly. We have had another one die in hospital, a Corporal from Sleaford.

We expect to be reviewed by Lord Bobs before we come home and are having a preliminary inspection today by the Captain. It does get hot here in the day time, unbearable sometimes but the nights are splendid.

A sergeant and three of our men got their discharges yesterday has they are going to stop in the country. What do you say if I stop on the new Railway job, sign on for two year at £1 a day and £500 when your time is up and act as a guard to the niggers while they work. But I like Old England best. The Regulars are wild because we are leaving first, the reserve men particularly, but we have a right to do, it is their trade and not ours. We tell them so and it does make them savage, it would have been a bad job for them if the Volunteers and Colonials had not helped them. In Nitrals Nek they did not show up very well, all there things were captured, but our Volunteers saved our waggon and their Maxim gun, the only waggon saved.

Dont let H Dickinson put this in print if you show him the letter. I think that is all this time.

Love to all at Sheffield, kiss baby and tell her I have bought her a nice little comb for her hair.

Remember me to all

With best love

Walter

Give W Skinner these stamps

The reference in the previous letter to some of the men being discharged to take up jobs in South Africa (see also Fig. 8) relates to Lord Milner's plans for the reconstruction period after the war.[8]

Walter's letters frequently comment, at this time, on the amount of illness among the troops. His company had already lost Fred Skinner to enteric fever; and Tom Hockney, although he had survived the fever, had been invalided home. Walter himself, although always complaining about his health, had suffered only minor bouts of illness, including the trouble with his ears which seriously affected his hearing. One suspects that Walter, the only son of a doting mother, was something of a hypochondriac.

In October 1900, the British public received the first intimation that all was not well with Queen Victoria's soldier grandson, Prince Christian Victor, the elder

Fig. 8. In South Africa with men, in civilian clothes, who had opted to stay and work in that country.

son of Princess Helena (Princess Christian of Schleswig-Holstein), the third daughter of the Queen. By the time the news was reported in the press, the Prince had already died. He was buried in Pretoria.

In 1904 the Princess Christian travelled to South Africa to visit her son's grave. She retained an interest in South Africa and became the President of the Nursing Committee of the South African Colonisation Society. She helped to recruit many nurses for the country.[9]

Lindsey and Lincolnshire Star, 27 October 1900, p. 6

PRINCE CHRISTIAN ILL

The eldest son of Princess Christian, on duty in South Africa, is suffering from enteric fever. He is attached to the King's Royal Rifles in which he has served since 1891.

Lindsey and Lincolnshire Star, 10 November 1900

PRINCE CHRISTIAN VICTOR'S FUNERAL
An Impressive Ceremony

8th October, Pretoria
The troops, arms reversed, lined the whole of the two miles of the route to the cemetery.
*   The march to the cemetery occupied, in all, two hours, and minute guns were booming for the whole of the time, a most impressive effect.*

As he reports in the following letter, Walter was one of the soldiers who lined the streets of Pretoria for the funeral of Prince Christian Victor.

Letter 30

Daspoort Range
Pretoria
Nov 7/1900

Dear Mother

I thought I would just drop another line or two, we are still here. We got another order a fortnight ago, to be ready at an hours notice and we still seem to be as far off as ever. We shall only have to stay another fortnight if we want to get home by Christmas. We are heartily sick of it, the suspence waiting every day for the order. Nearly all the other Volunteers have gone and Roberts and Buller have gone too. It is a miserable existence nothing but eating, drinking, work and sleep.

Our Company went to town the other day to line the streets while they were burying Prince Christian. I dont know whether you got the last letter or not. We heard De Wet had captured the mail. I sent some locust wings in it. We have had some heavy storms lately, it being the wet season now. The hills are beginning to look nice now with flowers and ferns, the birds have started laying. It gets light in a morning about four oclock and dark at six.

I am sorry to have missed the tradesmen prize shoot, has I always manage a prize but I think we are missing everything this year. You had better get a Christmas dinner ready to send out here. If you remember last year, I grated the carrots and bread for the pudding, wish I was doing the same this year. Well I hope to be in time to taste it, dont expect any more letters after this, the monotony is unbearable nearly. Up at half past five; bed any time after six, wont it be a treat to get undressed into a nice soft bed.

Well goodbye for the present. Remember me to all enquirers. Kiss May for Uncle, love to all at Sheffield.

With best love to you

Walter

On 6 November the Free State Commando, under Christiaan De Wet, was caught unawares by the British at Bothaville. Although De Wet managed to escape, the Commando suffered considerable losses of men and equipment. Such Boer setbacks convinced the ordinary soldier that the war was, indeed, virtually over. Although De Wet was back in action within the month, Walter and his comrades awaited, with confidence, the demobilisation not only of the Volunteers but of the whole British Army.

Letter 31

Daspoort Range
Pretoria
Nov 14/1900

Dear Mother

No signs yet of coming, but we are still under an hours notice. The reserves are [de]mobolising, it will be a bit thick if they start before us. Hockney is down at Wynberg Hospital, a suburb of Cape Town. We keep sending men to hospital. G. Peck and Teddy Cross from Brigg are both in.

We had a laugh when we saw about Freeman getting married. We all laid it out to the same cause that he had got her in the family way. Ill bet George Atkinson got drunk that night. Tell him I shall want a drink over the wedding when I get back, and tell him we do get a fair dinner when we get frozen meat instead of trek oxen. Tell Bill Betts to save some books to read, and you save the London Readers and Family Herald etc has I do miss the reading out here, and tell Bill Betts I have gone foreign but not to New South Wales, he will know what I means.

One of the buglers from Lincoln got on a horse yesterday to have a ride without bridle or saddle, the horse threw him onto the rocks and broke his jaw in two places, we picked him up unconscious, so he is all right for a month or six weeks.

The Captain has not given up hopes yet of being home for Christmas. We think it is owing to it being unsettled in the Orange River Colony. But De Wet has had a good cut up which no doubt you have seen. We see that General Buller has arrived. Us, the Hants and Norfolks are the only Volunteers left at Pretoria. We see three companies have sailed. Tell Freddy Middleton I hope to be in time for a drink at his house at Christmas just to keep old times up.

I think that is all this time. Remember me to all enquirers. Kiss May for me. Love to all at Sheffield
best love to you

Walter

I should think Jubby will want a coin to make Carrie a brooch with. One of our fellows sent a Kruger shilling to his wife, she sold it for seven shillings

Roll on England

While the Linconshire Volunteers waited for news of their demobilisation, they were chagrined to hear of the return home of other Volunteers and especially of the City Imperial Volunteers, the CIVs, the best known and the most lauded of the Volunteer battalions. Walter claimed to be 'sick of reading about them in the papers'.

Lindsey and Lincolnshire Star, 13 October 1900

CIVs EMBARK FOR ENGLAND

The CIVs arrived at Cape Town in special trains looking fit and well. An immense concourse of the people had assembled to give them welcome ... Sir A. Milner also visited the men after they had embarked ... and said that South Africa, in common with the rest of the Empire, owed them a deep debt of gratitude. The volunteers were loudly cheered and ... proceeded to the transport Aurania amid a scene of unbounded enthusiasm.

Much was made in the press of their arrival home. The *Lindsey and Lincolnshire Star* devoted most of a page to the celebrations in London under the following headlines.

Lindsey and Lincolnshire Star, 3 November 1900

SCENES AT SOUTHAMPTON

THE MARCH THROUGH LONDON

THE CITY'S GREETING

Judging by the following poem, found with the Barley letters, the general admiration of the CIVs was not entirely uncritical. The poem is printed as a single sheet without date or acknowledgement of source.

'THE IMMORTAL C.I.V.!'
By the Author of 'Section D'.

'Tis nigh on twelve long months ago, amidst the cannon's rattle,
When Cronje and his wily men fought Magersfontein battle.
When London heard of this reverse which caused our Empire tears,
'Let's raise a thousand men', said they, 'from our noble Volunteers'.

I saw them first at Jacobsdaal, in which they did their share,
At Paardeberg and Poplar Grove, their mounted men were there.
I saw some members of this band at the Battle of Karree,
Not on the flanks, nor in the van, but in the rear with me.

I was leading a mule, like a silly old fool, across hill, dale and moor,
When I saw some men, eating bread and jam, outside a farmhouse door.
I wondered why they lagged behind, and whoever they could be?
With their 'Smashers' and 'Brass Letters', 'the Immortal C.I.V.'

I saw them last upon parade in this famed town of forts,
They were sending them back to their city home, this band of 'Gentlemen
    Sports'.
We admire their deeds of valour, we liked their winsome ways,
We don't begrudge them what they won, their City's unstinted praise.

But will Pressmen please remember – though we have hearts of steel –
When they call them 'Tommy's superiors' we still have hearts that feel.
Some regiments here have lost their half amidst the din of battle,
The other half that's left to fight, are made of that same metal.

The end, alas! seems distant far, the war clouds still float o'er,
And many brave men still meet death, at the hands of marauding boer.
To find the cause, I need not seek, 'tis plain as plain can be,
We can't complete this war without 'The Immortal C.I.V.'!

Letter 32

Nov 27/1900
Daspoort Range
Pretoria

Dear Mother

Sorry to tell you we shall not get home for Christmas. I think they intend to make us stop our year, as according to other soldiers on active service they leave the country six weeks before their time is up, to allow them to get home, so by that we should get down to Cape Town by the 14th of Dec. We keep seeing other Volunteers are sailing by the papers, well I expect our turn will come shortly.

We hear that Hockney had been ordered home, we were glad to hear he was getting better, so he is lucky to get home for Christmas. We have been saving our tobacco but if he has come home we are going to smoke it, has we have only about $1/4$lb left. Get me a dozen bottles of beer in, as soon as you get this letter, then they will be in good condition, get them at Joe White's, Bass's Beer.

All our party are in good health now. All our Officers are laid up again, Lieutenant Lee has been invalided home. I see the C.I.V.s had a month's furlough and a month's pay. We are sick of reading about them in the papers. Anybody would think they were the only Volunteers that had been out. The Cape Town Highlanders I see have been cut up, they were stationed with us at Tulbagh. One or two I knew were killed too. One that was in the Jameson Raid was killed too.

I have got more thorns to bring home. I should not have wrote if it had not been to wish you a Merry Christmas. Well remember me to everybody. I think I shall get back in time for Spring Cleaning. This is the last sheet of paper I have and had to borrow the stamp so dont expect more letters.

Well goodbye for the present. Wishing you all a Merry Christmas and a Happy New Year, with best love to you all.

Walter

Kiss the children for me.

You see the stamp on the envelope, the money is made like that on one side and Kruger's head on the other.

Hull Times, 17 November 1900, p. 7

THE 'TREATING' OF SOLDIERS
To the Editor of the 'Hull Times'

SIR, – May I be allowed more particularly to call attention of the public to the paragraph in Lord Roberts' appeal, in which our great General expresses 'his sincere hope that the welcome may not take the form of "treating" the men to stimulants in public houses or in the streets, and thus lead them to excesses which must tend to degrade those whom the nation delights to honour, and to lower the "Soldiers of the Queen" in the eyes of the world – that world which has watched with undisguised admiration the grand work they have performed for their Sovereign and their country'.

Such are the words of Lord Roberts, who has done and suffered so much for his country. Can we show our gratitude to him in any better way than by taking his words to heart and obeying them? –

I am, Sir, etc
W. LATHAM COX, *Major*
Commanding Depot, Lincolnshire Regiment, Lincoln

November 14th 1900

Lindsey and Lincolnshire Star, 8 December 1900, p. 5

RETURN OF ONE OF THE VOLUNTEERS

Scunthorpe gave Pte Hockney a grand reception on Thursday night on his return from South Africa from whence he had been invalided and sent in advance of the other members. It was not known until late in the afternoon that he was coming, but Col/Sgt Fowler mustered a good contingent of the men.

When the train rushed in Private Hockney was lustily cheered ...

A noticeable feature was the respect paid to Lord Roberts' appeal that there should be no treating to alcohol and there was no halt made at the public houses.

Letter 33

Dasspoort Range
Pretoria
Dec 13/1900

Dear Mother

Just a few lines to tell you that things are all right. I did not get Hull Times last mail so perhaps he has stopped sending them but I saw the Barton Times, it is a very good paper. I was surprised to see such information in it. Dont forget to get my watch mended, you know what it wants doing to.

Christmas Day we are getting 3/- given to us, to buy something for our dinners. We are doing very nicely now, the Hindoos bring their baskets up, and sell us things, cakes, four for sixpence, cucumbers 3 for a 1/-, they are shorter than ours and thicker. Then onions and tomatoes, and vinegar 1/- per pint, monkey nuts, you get as many at home for a penny has we get for sixpence. They always roast them here, you maybe think they grow on the monkey nut tree, but they dont, they grow like potatoes.

It is very hot now being summer time, it is generally 100 degrees before breakfast. We could not understand it the other morning, the sun was shining and it was cool. When we looked at it there was a big spot on it, so perhaps you could not see it in England.

Dont let these letters get in the paper. Dickinson put in about those two games of billiards that I had. He said I had took down all comers and you know I never said anything of the sort, our fellows got on to me about it.

There are some splendid butterflies here, anyone could make a good collection. I often find birds nests in the kopjes, but a singular thing about the birds is, they never whistle.

Rhodes has dysentry and is passing blood, he has just been to the doctor who has sent him to the hospital. Drury has been ill, but is better, so we have all been ill except Marris. Well about coming home, we seem to be has far off as ever, so we have settled down and letting things take their course, hoping to see you before long, dont care how soon.

Remember me to all enquirers, hoping to be in time for some bug blinding

Love to all at Sheffield and you

Walter

A Happy New Year to you all

Postscript on a separate scrap of paper.

When you write tell me if you had any money from the fund because
it said in the Hull Times that only £11 had been given locally because
I understood from Alec that you and Polly were getting 15/- a week

Letter 34

Boxing Day
Daspoort Range
Pretoria

Dear Mother

I thought I had about finished writing but it seems not. How did
you enjoy Christmas. We did very well through the kindness of a
Gentleman at Cape Town, who used to live at Boston. He sent Plum
Puddings, some Juice Cordial, Jam, $^1/_4$lb tobacco and 20 cigarettes
each and biscuits, and then with the 3/6 we were allowed, we had a
good feed. Breakfast, cocoa, milk, butter, Salmon, Lobster, Sardines,
Cucumber. Dinner, Beef, Mutton, Pickles, Plum Puddings, Rum Sauce
and a pint of beer each. Tea, Cake, splendid too, jam, cheese and
biscuits so you see we had a good time, but then it was not like being
at home, the beer too as thin as it could be. Fancy eight months
without booze.

The Captain gave it out on Church Parade, Christmas Day that an
Army order had come out – All Volunteers to serve 12 months in
South Africa, if that is so we have to stop while the 16th of March, of
course, that is the latest they can keep us, or does it mean by the 25th
of Jan when we joined. Of course we were on active or foreign service
when we left Southampton, well hoping the time is short now.

There was a rumour that the Boers were going to take Pretoria on
Christmas Day, so of course we were up by three oclock, stood to
arms while five, nice thing to be up on Christmas Day and no beer,
wasnt it. Ten of our Company had to go to escort a convoy last Friday
to Rietfontein, past Nitrals Nek. Marris was the only one out of our
lot that went. We are having a lot of sickness now among the men,
another has died, which makes seven we have lost now and three or
four more gone into hospital this week. We have not heard how
Rhodes is.

If you do not hear about us coming home when you get this, write
and let me know how things are and send me a paper or two, such as

Answers or Pearsons Weekly anything like that. If I dont receive them it will only be a few coppers wasted. I am afraid to send any money home has Alec sent Polly 3 separate Sovereigns and she has not received them. I see they are going to have a drinking fountain, we shall have to look sharp or it will be up before we get home.

Well I think that is all this time so remember me to all enquirers, love to all at Sheffield, best love to yourself

Walter

Kiss May for uncle

Happy New Year

The following clipping, recording an interview with one of the colonial volunteers from Australia, was found with the letters. It is not dated and the name of the source has been mutilated but reads – [Tel]egraph and Star.

A CHRISTMAS ON THE VELDT
TROOPER'S POETICAL DESCRIPTION
Bully Beef, Biscuits and Dreams

Private Maxwell of the New South Wales Mounted Infantry, who is just now in Liverpool, has been telling an interviewer that he spent last Christmas among the kopjes and the veldt.

'I presume you remember well what it was like?' he was asked.

'I do, and if I were to spend a century more of Christmases on this earth I should never forget it.'

'Had you any Christmas fare at all?'

'Not a particle, and we looked for none; we had to look to our horses, our guns and our lives. Eating was off, except for the rations we were glad to get to keep the life within us. The climate of the Transvaal is a beautiful one, and it was pleasant even in the dead of night to stand behind a kopje or a trench, and watch the gradual sinking of the sun on Christmas Eve, over the long veldt, and straggling hills. The night came on and Christmas Eve slowly, gradually, quietly, insensibly mingled with Christmas morn. There was a dread silence in camp; many were sleeping, but many more were waking – thinking, thinking – dreaming under that glittering, starry dome, of home and happiness, of friend and wife and child, of mistletoe bough and fair eyes. And our teeth', he went on, 'watered occasionally as we thought of the viands on the table, though our

thoughts as a rule turned little in that way ... I was thinking of the bullets that came whizzing past on that Christmas watch. Some of them as near as they could well get without actually finding billets – and sometimes the billets were found. Many a gallant fellow went down that Christmas week, sinking to rise no more, but neither the sight of those who fell nor the privations we underwent – nothing ever made us falter in our devotion to Old England. By the stars that shone above us, and the love we carried in our hearts, with all its awakening emotions, by the memories of Christmas times, and the memories of a thousand things sacred to us, we silently swore in our hearts that Christmas that we would fight and die for the honour of the flag, and hand it down unstained – fluttering in its glory and its joy – to our descendants. Loneliness and a great cause made the commonest of us work and fight like Trojans.'

'And how about that last Christmas dinner on the kopjes – what was it?'

'Nothing but bully beef.'

'With nothing to wash it down?'

'Nothing liquid except a fond – and perhaps an unhidden – tear for those far away, and ...'

Here the brave fellow faltered, the memory being over-charged with thought.

MEANWHILE ...

September to December 1900

During September and October, while the Regular Army was capturing Prinsloo in the Brandwater Basin and then pursuing De Wet and Botha, Walter and the Volunteers were guarding the mountains to the north of Pretoria against possible Boer attack. Still convinced that a declaration of peace was imminent, as he had reported on and even witnessed the surrender of groups of Boers, Walter's attention turned towards an early return home. The weeks, however, dragged on with no sign of the hoped-for demobilisation, even when, in the middle of October, the City Imperial Volunteers entrained for Cape Town on the first leg of their journey home.

In November the health risks to the troops were poignantly underlined with the death from enteric fever of Queen Victoria's grandson, Prince Christian Victor.

Walter's Company had already suffered their own loss on 12 July when Fred Skinner died of the same disease. Fred must have been very much in their thoughts on 8 November as the Lincolnshire Volunteers lined the streets of Pretoria for the funeral of the Prince.

November saw dissension on both sides. Roberts had convinced himself and the British Government that the Boers were on the point of final collapse. He was supported in this belief by Kitchener and, as a result, many army units, both regular and volunteer, including the City Imperial Volunteers, were repatriated. Having noted that, by their guerrilla tactics, De la Rey was reclaiming parts of south-eastern Transvaal and De Wet was continuing to take both supplies and prisoners on both sides of the Vaal River, Milner strongly disagreed.

On the Boer side, when the leaders had met in late October at the remote farm of Cypherfontein in Western Transvaal, some had argued against the guerrilla war on the grounds of both logistics and morality. Botha, particularly, as Walter commented, was doubtful of the outcome as the retributive burning of farmsteads and the displacement of Boer civilians intensified. The answer seemed to be a joint invasion of Natal and the Cape, but the rifts between the Transvaalers and the Free Staters were too deep and the commandos began to disperse.

On 6 November, Steyn and De Wet received what Walter called 'a good cut up' at Bothaville, losing all their artillery and many men. The leaders escaped only because of the slowness of the British column. This success was not, however, followed up and, by early December, the regrouped commandos were back to attacking British supply lines. On the 12th the British suffered a major defeat when De la Rey and Jan Smuts ambushed Clements at an ill-chosen campsite in the mountains to the west of Pretoria. Clements managed to escape with half of his men and all his guns but it was a warning of the success of the Boer tactics.

As the year drew to a close, the initiative was retrieved by the British, and the Boers, in desperation, turned their eyes to Cape Province in the hope of an Afrikaner uprising there.

Chapter 9

In Action Again

January to February 1901

> *Out o' the wilderness, 'dusty an' dry*
>   (Time, an' 'igh time to be trekkin' again!)
> *'Oo is it 'eads to the Detail Supply?*
>   (A section, a pompom, an' six 'undred men.)
>
>   Kipling – 'Columns'

As Walter and his comrades waited impatiently for the order to begin the journey home the war was, in fact, entering a new phase. The controversial 'scorched earth' policy operated by the British Army, with the intention of depriving the Boer commandos of their home bases and, thereby, of food, arms stockpiles and remounts, had begun the previous July on the orders of Lord Roberts. Later he had begun to doubt its value as it appeared only to strengthen the resolve of the Boers to fight on, but it was intensified by Kitchener after Roberts's departure.

The following reports in the local press seem to have been published as a justification for the treatment meted out to Boer women and children. Readers in Britain, no doubt, would have been led to the conclusion not only that the strategy was militarily necessary but that the Boer population deserved the reprisals for their 'treachery'. It was not until later in the year that protests by Emily Hobhouse against the destruction and the camps began to change the attitude of the British public to the policy.

Walter makes no reference to farm-burning, but other reports from soldiers and correspondents noted the burning of Boer farms and the removal of women and children to the 'refuges' that became known as 'concentration camps'.

Lindsey and Lincolnshire Star, 22 September 1900, p. 6

MORE BOER TREACHERY

From Lord Roberts to the War Office.
'*Hillyard telegraphing from Utrecht states that on the 15th a party of
13th Hussars patrolling 10 miles west of Utrecht were invited by some
women into a farm over which a white flag was flying. The patrol
were offered some milk and bread and as they were leaving the house
were fired upon. The farm, which belonged to A. Venter, field cornet
of Utrecht, the leader of the late raids on the railway, was destroyed.
A similar act of treachery occurred near Commando Nek a day or two
ago when a man of Paget's Horse was killed.*'

Lindsey and Lincolnshire Star, 12 January 1901, p. 6

HERTZOG SICK OF THE WAR

*Reuter reports on invading parties of Boers into Cape Colony and
measures to repel them. Carnarvon, Commandant, reports that
Hertzog has declared that he is very sick of guerrilla war but that
Pretorius is determined to continue. All farmers on line of route have
suffered severe loss at their hands ...*
   '*The country around Kimberley is being cleared of people,
livestock and foodstuffs and women and children are being brought
in.*'

The following story was repeated, with variations, so often that it is difficult not
to assume that it was apocryphal and served a propaganda purpose.

Lindsey and Lincolnshire Star, 23 March 1901, p. 3

BOER SLIMNESS[10]

*The manner in which innocent-looking farm houses were used by the
Boers for storing arms and ammunition was illustrated by T.F. Best,
Canadian YMCA repesentative in South Africa ... 'One day we
accompanied a party of scouts to a farm house tenanted only by*

118

women. They denied that there were any arms in the house but a search revealed six hidden rifles. Finally suspicion fell on one of the women who, it was noticed, never stirred from her seat. She was made to rise and concealed under the stool and the folds of her dress were discovered several thousand rounds of ammunition.' The soldiers, Mr Best said, felt no regrets as the place went up in smoke and had no sympathy for the treacherous women.

Lindsey and Lincolnshire Star, 6 April 1901, p. 3

BRITISH COLUMNS ACTIVE

Standerton – The British columns in the East Transvaal have resumed operations after 6 weeks of inactivity, due mainly to the incessant rains. Our men are sweeping the country clear of everything that might be of use to the Boers ...

This policy, however deplorable, is demanded by the stern necessity of war, but all the Boer women and children have been well cared for by our troops. The enemy show their gratitude by persevering in their resistance unhampered by the impediment of womenfolk.

The last British convoy to Utrecht safely conveyed 500 members of Boer families to the town where they will find better accommodation and their wants well attended to.

Letter 35

This is one of Walter's longest letters and shows the extent to which his literacy had improved from the first hesitant letters of a year earlier.

Jouberts Farm
Near Rietfontein
Jan 9/1901

Dear Mother

You will think it strange me not writing before, but we have had to go on the trek again. We started Saturday after Xmas about four in the afternoon, marched to West Fort about 7 miles, w[h]ere we camped for the night. Sunday went to Rietfontein, which is opposite Nitrals Nek, stayed there the night, Monday went over Crocodile

River, through Commando Nek on the Magelesburg Range to Bokfontein. Tuesday went to Wolhootens Kop to join Clements Force, about 1700 cavalry and a lot of infantry. There were about 8000 boers about 10 mile off. Thursday morning we started about two, to take a convoy, made the front of it a dummy one, as we expected the boers to attack, has they have no supplies. All the troops went, but when they saw us coming they scooted. We went through with it to Elands Drift where another party took it over. We camped there the night and came back to Wolhootens Kop, next morning. At night another convoy came and wanted a company to guard them through the thick brushwood, of course it was our luck to have to go. After seeing that through we all came back to Rietfontein, where we arrived on the Sunday.

All the Regiment are camping there. It had been a heavy week not much sleep, through being on outpost and being wet through nearly every day, and our clothes has to dry on, and I have only one shirt, it has not been washed for a month, and I have to fasten my trousers together with bits of string, has they are all in pieces, but one good thing, we have plenty of bully beef, biscuits and jam.

Well we thought we had earned a rest, but on Tuesday morning we were called up at 2 oclock. Paget wanted two of our companies to make a battalion, to march down the valley about twenty miles, to intercept the Boers if they broke through Plummers two brigades. French was driving them in, the first night we camped here at Jouberts Farm, w[h]ere we had a good feed in the orched. Peaches, apples, grapes, pomegranites, quinces and prickly pears.

Wednesday we started about 3 (which was going to be a day of events) we marched about eight miles to Schuberts Kop. When the boers on the hills opened fire we formed for attack, and our guns started shelling them, and about two companies opened fire and kept it up while the baggage got past, the bullets were flying about, we then followed the baggage, and camped about four mile further on, five of our scouts got captured.

After being in camp about a hour we found our waggon had not turned up, so our company had to fall in and go back. We saw our waggon w[h]ere the boers attacked, with nobody with it, against some farms. We could not understand it, while we got within 500 yards and then we knew, the boers opened fire on us, and we were out in the open. They had come down off the hills, it was as warm as hell for about 100 yds while we reached the houses It was a marvellous thing but not one was hit, and the bullets were whistling and screaming around us. The baggage guard (Alec and Drury were two of them) said after we had got past, they opened fire on them, they being behind us owing to the waggon sticking in a drift. They had to leave the waggon and seek cover behind a wall, they peppered the waggon well as bullets were found in the blankets. Well then we formed in single rank 6 paces extend in front of the waggon, and opened fire while the waggon went on, when it was safe the big guns opened fire while we retired, we fell back on the camp and had tea.

There were 400 boers, 11 were killed and 17 wounded, our loss was one mule wounded. After a rest we were ordered back to Jouberts Farm. Well luck was with us again, the waggon got stuck in the sand, after about an hour at it we got it out, then about half a mile further on, the hind wheel broke in pieces. An ambulance waggon came and took what it could, the rest we had to abandon, so the boers would get that. We arrived at the farm about 1 oclock, after a hard days work and over twenty miles marching.

Thursday. I have just had a good feed off prickly pears, so thought I would write a bit, it is the first chance we have had. We stayed here two nights then moved about two miles from the farm, w[h]ere we are in ambush in front of a pass. One of our Colonial Scouts was killed by a sniper within a few yards of our camp.

Monday we started for Reitfontein the Boers having got through somehow in the night, so it was no use staying and Paget had gone on to Pretoria to get refitted and new remounts. We camped at Rietfontein at night and next morning we got orders to take H Company's place on the kopjes of Daspoort Range about twenty miles from Pretoria, where we are going to stay till we go home. We have to be at home by the 16th of March so we shall only have about three weeks or a month to do for a blessing. We have four hours a day fatigue work to do, but we have plenty of food, has Reitfontein is a base supply for stores.

I see Hockney has arrived, let him see this letter. I think that is all this time. Remember me to all enquirers. Love to all at Sheffield. Kiss May for uncle, with best love

Walter

Roll on England
Don't forget that beer
I have just been making some jam out of peaches and sugar as I am on observation.

Hoping you are all well as I am

Walter Marris also wrote home about the events at Joubert's Farm. His letters were printed in the local paper.

Lindsey and Lincolnshire Star, 23 May 1901, p. 5

THE SCUNTHORPE VOLUNTEERS IN SOUTH AFRICA

Daspoort – Pte Walter Marris to his parents.
'We left Pretoria on December 29th after having a pretty fair Christmas. We went out as the intention of relieving the 5th Northumberland Fusiliers at Commando Nek 25 miles from Pretoria, but when we got there we received fresh orders to join Clement's Company at Waluter's Kop on the Rustenburg Road. On 3rd January we advanced again for Delary (De la Rey) who was reported to be entrenched at Eland's Kop 10 miles away. We were up at midnight and marching off at 1 am – we got there at daybreak to find that they had cleared off as usual … We thought we were in for a "scrap" and a capture but our movement was a failure. We got back to Rietfontein on the 6th. We were up at 2 am on the 8th and went to join Paget's force. We advanced up to Crocodile Valley and came under fire on the 9th – not very heavy. Our guns put 8" shells into them and then we advanced and camped three miles past where we had been fighting and waited for our baggage to come up. It didn't turn up so our company went for it. When we got to where we had been fighting before, the Boers opened fire on us again all of a sudden and quite surprised us. We made all haste for the wagon which was then about 3/4 of a mile away. They gave it to us blooming hot all the way to the wagon which we found stuck fast in the sand. When we got there we all took cover on a farm until reinforcement came. It was no good us trying with the wagon under heavy fire and unseen enemy. Two guns and the active company of Lincolns came to our assistance. We got the wagon out of the range of the enemy but the enemy kept up a stack firing all the time. When we got back to camp again we received orders to proceed to Grobler's Farm 10 miles off. We marched off at 10.30 in extended order about 10,000 yards in front of the hill where the Boers had been firing on us. We covered all the baggage past us and also Plummer's Horse which had joined us at night. We went on about 1000 yards and then our wagon stuck fast. We all got round it and pushed for all we were worth and the axle broke and over went the wagon. We were then in a fix but set to work to unload the wagon and got orders to carry our kits but didn't carry them far as they stopped an*

ambulance wagon and loaded it up. Some men lost everything they had including curios they had collected. We landed at camp at 1.30 pm after what I call a hard day's work.

'We thought our time was up in January but it seems they can do *what they like with us. We came out when they were hard pressed and sacrificed everything and they can afford to let the regular troops come home. How is it they can't let us go also? We would not like to leave a job half finished. The sending home of troops in October was all an election game just to stuff it into the people that the war was over.'*[11]

27 January – Marris reported that they were – Guarding the bridge at Crocodile River and better off than before. They could get a wash. They had been up on the hill for eight days with only one wash and that in a mess tin. Hopes to be home by mid-April after 12 months in the country.

Letter 36

The baby mentioned in the following letter was Molly, my mother. She was fifteen months old at the time and Lenna must have complained about her in the letter mentioned by Walter. Molly was always sensitive about her position in the family, being the fifth girl in a row, so I never showed her this letter.

From the context of the mention of George Jubb we must assume that he had married his fiancée, Carrie.

Jan 16th

Dear Lillie,

I have just received your letters and very pleased too to get some. Tell George its a mucky trick not waiting while I got home. Ill give him it. You need not be frightened about a Dutch girl, they are plain beggars.

My word Lenna can write. I should not have thought it. Tell her I shall give her a Kruger penny for passing her examination and we shall be home in eight weeks time if we are alive, and tell her I shall turn that baby out when I come. I think we are a dirty colour now, but perhaps we shall bleach coming across the water. They tell me I look a lot older. Tell Charlie I am living in hopes of that beer after 9 months without any.

Love to all

Walter

Letter 37

This is the first to be written on one of the blue Letter Cards issued to the troops. Walter appears to have miscalculated how much he could write on one as there is no ending to the letter. It arrived at Scunthorpe on 25 February 1901.

Jan 29/1901
Bait Hill

Dear Mother

We are still on this hill, half of us, the other half is in a redoubt about 3 miles off. There are about 27 of us to hold about a mile and half of kopjes, we can see the boers opposite. We call this Bait Hill has we are nothing but a bait, and to make things better the captain sends two parties of us, three in each party, in the morning before we come off outpost, to the bottom of the hill, to patrol amongst the bushes, to see if there are any boers lurking about. We start just before daylight, it takes about an hour and half, if there was any there they could pop us off nicely. It is a wild looking country here at the foot of the hill, there is Piet Pretorius Garden, plenty of pears, peaches and prickly pears.

We have been having a lot of sickness, two more have died this week, and several bad in hospital. Half of the company have got veldt sores, they are bad, they eat into your hand if not attended to. I have only had one, which is getting better. Charlesworth and Drury have them. Marris seems to escape everything. We hear Rhodes has gone down country, so that shows he is nearly better.

Letter 38

Pages 2 to 4 of an incomplete letter. No date but about the end of January 1901. This fragment was given to me by May.

... we have plenty of work here, outpost every other night, and from four hours fatigue every day. This post is supposed to be relieved every ten days or a fortnight, to give the men a rest, but we have been here nearly three weeks but of course we are only Volunteers and they are taking it out of us. It is always Volunteers if work wants doing. Our captain says we are the only Volunteer Company at the front.

We heard yesterday that Baden Powel was going to take the

valley over with 500 police, we are hoping so. We do not get much water, it has to be carried up in barrels by mules. We have evacuated Nitrals Nek, Bokfontein, Wolhootens Kop etc and they are occupied by boers. We think there is a big move on and that is only a trap to get the boers in, so we are surrounded except for Pretoria way, and we should look healthy with 27 men if they attacked. We heard that Kitchener said, the boers had tried several times to take Rietfontein, but he would make them attack now, so it looks as if there were a force driving them with being so near us.

We are living better than we did at Pretoria, and we can buy milk, sugar, flour, herrings and quaker oats, tobacco English. We have to buy them wholesale a case at a time, we do have a blow out on quaker oats made with milk, they are splendid, 9d a packet.

We have made a blockhouse and Major Day says if the boers attack we have to hold it at all costs, and we have made barbed wire entanglements on the hill side so they would get a warm reception, we can see them across the valley, bringing their horses to water. Our Captain is sick again. We can manage very well without him, he never studies the mens comfort, he always tried to put more work on, not a man in the company likes him, but thank the Lord there will only be three more weeks after you receive this, so dont write again after this. You can show Dickinson the last letter, with our fight in, disease is more to be feared than bullets. I have kept myself all right with Beechams Pills, I take one very night.

Well I think that is all the news this time. Have you enjoyed Christmas. We did very well under the circumstances. We keep reckoning every day another day nearer home. I see Hockney is doing very well, remember us to him, me and Drury is on this hill, Marris and Charlesworth is at the Redoubt. We have about 60 niggers working here.

Remember me to all enquirers. Kiss May for Uncle, love to all at Sheffield. I expect you are there now. Goodbye for the present

With best love

Walter

Letter 39

The ostrich feathers mentioned in this letter were in May's possession until she was forced by increasing infirmity, in her late 80s, to give up her home.

Feb 7/1901
Rietfontein
Dear Mother
Nothing particular to write about. We are still on these kopjes, expecting every day to be relieved has a draft is leaving Pretoria and we are going to headquarters here.

I have sent some ostrich feathers for Kate and Lillie, 1 feather and 1 pair of tips each. I have not sent you any has I thought they would not suit a woman of your age, so I have sent them giddy young girls them. I dont know what to buy you, but I will see when we get into a town again.

Only another 5 weeks here for a blessing. Three niggers were shot here by the boers yesterday.

Love to all at Sheffield. Remember me to all, with best love
Walter
Both the Captain (Stephenson) and Lieut Dickenson are in hospital. Lieut came with draft.

While Walter and his companions were waiting daily for news of their demobilisation, plans were being debated in Scunthorpe for suitable ways of commemorating the war service and return of the local men. Local rivalries obviously ran deep when considering matters such as these!

Hull Times, 24 November 1900, p. 7

THE RETURNING VOLUNTEERS
SUGGESTED MEMORIAL AT SCUNTHORPE

On Monday, a largely attended meeting was held in the Assembly Rooms, Scunthorpe. It was called by Mr J. Fletcher, J.P., chairman of the Urban District Council, to consider what steps should be taken to provide a public memorial to the Volunteers and Reservists who went from the district to serve in South Africa, and who are shortly returning home.

Mr Fletcher presided, and in opening the meeting said that the Vicar of the parish, the Rev. H.L. Ashdown, had expressed disappointment at not being able to be present, but the project had his sympathy. The chairman went on to say that this memorial was independent of the action taken by the Peace Celebration Committee, which had suspended their labours for a while. It had been suggested that the memorial take the form of a drinking fountain, the names of the Volunteers and Reservists to be inscribed upon it. The chairman then referred specially to the services of the Volunteers. It was purely a voluntary service, and differed in that way from the Reservists and the regulars. It was our patriotism arising from their desire to do their duty to Queen and country. With regard to the local fund, which had been subscribed to since the war broke out, Mr Edgar Brown had furnished him with a statement of the receipts and expenditure. The amount subscribed in Scunthorpe and district was £240 18s 5d, and of this sum there had been forwarded to the Central Fund of the Soldiers' and Sailors' Families Association £220. There had been paid locally £11, and there was a balance in the local treasurer's hands of £9 18s 5d. He thought the result was extremely satisfactory. (Cheers)

Captain Dove said the only suggestion, as far as he knew, was the one referred to by the chairman. He thought it admirable. At present there was no monument in the town, and nothing in the way of ornamentation of a public character. He dwelt upon the importance of the town; it had the highest rateable value, and the biggest population in the North Lindsey Division. The chairman had referred to the services of the Volunteers, and he endorsed all Mr Fletcher had said. It was an honour to the town to furnish so many man to serve with the colours.

Mr C.A. Cheesman supported the idea, and asked if anyone would give an estimate of the cost.

Mr H.S. Mcintosh said the suggestion was excellent. They could not give their heroes the freedom of the borough, but he suggested that all the soldiers that served with the colours belonging the district, as well as the Volunteers and Regulars, have their names inscribed upon the memorial.

Mr A. Shelton thought Scunthorpe was to get all the credit for the work done by the Frodingham Volunteers.

The Chairman said he was only acting for Scunthorpe that night. He had no power to call a meeting for Frodingham.

Mr F. Smith gave the scheme his support.

Mr G.W. Alcock thought Frodingham had borne the brunt of the work, and it was only right it should be taken into consideration. He referred to the death of Private Skinner, who was a Frodingham man.

Captain Dove pointed out that, subject to the Vicar's permission, the Volunteers proposed to erect a brass memorial tablet in Frodingham church to Skinner's memory.

Mr Walter Crook thought that so long as they did something to honour the men, the men would not mind whether it was erected in Scunthorpe or Frodingham.

Captain Dove said they ought to spend £250 and make a good job, or nothing at all.

Mr F. Stuffin thought that the two places ought to combine. Of course they always looked to Scunthorpe to take the lead, but it was a pity the chairmen of both Councils had not met and called a joint meeting.

Colour Sergeant Geary said if they called it a district memorial it would meet the case.

Mr J. Fowler proposed that a memorial be erected in Scunthorpe, and that the names of the Volunteers, Reservists, and Regulars who served in the South African War be inscribed thereon. This on being seconded, was carried unanimously.

Mr R.I. Swaby then proposed that the memorial take the form of a drinking fountain. Mr T.U. Chamberlain seconded and this motion was carried unanimously.

The following committee was then elected to ascertain the most suitable site, probable cost, and report to another meeting:- Mr J. Fletcher, Captain Dove, Lieut. B. Cliff, Messrs W. Woodley, W. Crooke, F. Stuffin, A. Hollingsworth, J. Long, G.W. Alcock, R.D. Lockwood, W. Gibson and Sergeant Instructor Bugg. Mr Fowler was elected secretary pro. tem.

MEANWHILE …

January to February 1901

In early January 1901 Walter was engaged in the only serious bout of fighting of his war. On the 9th he wrote to his mother a most detailed account of an engagement with the enemy. It is to Walter Marris, however, that we must turn for precise details of the brush with De la Rey's commando in the mountains to the north-west of Pretoria. The encounter was too small to receive coverage in the history books but was typical of the continuing guerrilla warfare by which the commandos tied down and engaged large numbers of British troops and then, after a brief engagement, slipped away.

In retaliation for the Boer raids, Kitchener began a series of drives against the commandos which also included sweeping up Boer women and children.

Chapter 10

Homeward Bound at Last

February to May 1901

> Me that 'ave been what I've been,
> Me that 'ave gone where I've gone,
> Me that 'ave seen what I've seen –
>   'Ow can I ever take on
> With awful old England again,
> An' 'ouses both sides of the street,
> And 'edges two sides of the lane,
> And the parson an' 'gentry' between,
> An' touchin' my 'at when we meet –
>   Me that 'ave been what I've been?
>
>   Kipling – 'Chant-Pagan'

The returning Volunteers would, no doubt, have mixed feelings when they returned home and set about readjusting to small-town England, after the excitements and dangers of their service in South Africa. But first there was the welcome and pageantry of their return. These events were made much of in the local papers.

Letter 40

Rietfontein
Feb 13/1901

Dear Mother

We have left the hills and are now at headquarters, expecting any day to be called to Pretoria for home. They have signalled on the heliograph from Pretoria wanting to know what we are doing here.

Two niggers were sjambocked[12] the other day, and sentenced to 2 years hard labour for driving cattle to the boers. They fetched pieces out of them. They call this valley the valley of death, as all horses and mules dies in it at this time of year. Three died against me the other night, while on guard at the Artillery Camp.

Well we expect to be at home by Good Friday at the latest, so get prepared to make a bit of fuss. I got your last letter, it cheers us all up to get one. Love to all at Sheffield. I thought A Threadgould could not live without Miss Roylance.

Goodbye for the present, with best love,
Walter

Letter 41

Rietfontein Hospital
March 25/1901

Dear Mother

Just a few lines to tell you I am all right, except twisted my knee a bit and am moving to the other hospital situated in Nitrals Nek and am going to stay there while we come home. Well we expected leaving on the 16th, we sent word to headquarters at Pretoria. They sent the message on to Kitchener. He said we had to stop while the other Volunteers that is coming out relieved us, we dont know when they sailed and cant get to know. We sent a cablegram a week since and have had no answer. We are waiting anxiously for them coming.

Lena Greens brother is here. You may expect us home a month after they reach here, about Whitsuntide.

Love to all at Sheffield, have no more paper.

With best love,
Walter

Get garden set again

In the following news item, the relieving Volunteers were reported to have proceeded to Grantham for training. If they sailed on 23 March as Walter believed, it would be at least a month before they could be expected in Pretoria. In the event the authorities decided to release the Lincolnshire Volunteers, who were, by whatever calculation was employed, well over the twelve months for which they had been contracted. The method of calculating the term of service was always vague. It was never clear whether the period of service started from the day of enlistment, from the day of embarkation or from the date of arrival in South Africa. Walter claimed that they were the only group not to have been repatriated, although it is not clear why this should have been so.

Lindsey and Lincolnshire Star, 16 February 1901, p. 5

FOR THE FRONT

On Wednesday morning members of G & H Company 3rd Volunteer Battalion Line Regiment left by train for Grantham for inspection, having volunteered for active service in South Africa.

Letter 42

Rietfontein
April 4/1901
Dear Mother
We are leaving here Friday morning at six for Pretoria for home. We are not waiting for the other Volunteers, we heard they sailed 23rd of March so they wont be here yet, I pity them, so we are expecting to be home ready for the Statutes.

We have a fortnights mail just come in, but I dont know whether there is anything for me or not, has I have to post this at once to catch the mail. I have had to borrow paper and envelope to write this. I have nothing more to tell you.

Love to all at Sheffield, remember me to all, dont forget the bottles of beer.
With best love
Walter

Lindsey and Lincolnshire Star, 11 May 1901, p. 5

VOLUNTEERS' HOMECOMING

At a meeting of the committee it was decided to present each man with a gold medal suitably inscribed. It was resolved to have a parade of the Volunteers and escort the returning warriors round the town. There will be a short thanksgiving service at the Parish Church the same evening. There will be a dinner in their honour the second day after their arrival with a public ball the night after.

Lindsey and Lincolnshire Star, 18 May 1901, p. 5

THE LANDING OF THE VOLUNTEERS

The news of the arrival of the home-coming Volunteers reached Scunthorpe on Thursday morning in a telegram from A. Charlesworth to John Fowler. The men will be entertained on Saturday afternoon at HQ, Lincoln and will arrive at Scunthorpe on the 6 pm train from Doncaster, when they will be given a hearty welcome.

The Lincolnshire Volunteers finally reached their homes on Saturday 23 May, a week after May's fourth birthday. Although she lived into her nineties, she never forgot the excitement of that day.

The festivities started at Lincoln, the headquarters of the Lincolnshire Regiment. The men were disbanded there before travelling by train to Doncaster, where they changed onto the Scunthorpe line. The festivities continued along the railway line as each group of men left the train at their home station.

Lindsey and Lincolnshire Star, 25 May 1901, p. 5

IN HONOUR OF BRAVE MEN
THE LINCOLNSHIRE VOLUNTEERS' RETURN HOME

Enthusiastic Receptions – Public Festivities and Banquets – General Holiday at Brigg, Barton, Gainsboro', Grimsby and Scunthorpe – Presentations to the Men
(Special Reports By Our Own Correspondents)

FESTIVITIES AT LINCOLN

On Thursday Lincoln was a city of rejoicing. The streets blossomed forth with flags and bunting; motor cars and trams were adorned with Union Jacks; the church bells rang and the school children were given a holiday. All day long the excitement grew and, when at length the Lincolnshire Volunteer heroes arrived, the excitement culminated in a general outburst of frantic enthusiasm, the memorable midnight send-off which the Volunteers received fifteen months ago being utterly eclipsed by the grandeur of their welcome home.

The train left Southampton at 10.38 and was not due to Lincoln until 6.20 and it arrived about 20 minutes late. The station yard was by then crowded with a surging multitude and the main street was packed. The cheers that rent the air as the khaki-clad heros made their appearance was deafening and almost drowned the band as it played 'Home Sweet Home'.

The Mayor, who was attired in his civic robes and was accompanied by the Sheriff, Bishop and Corporation, then mounted a specially prepared platform in the centre of the great area and bade the men a hearty welcome, informing them the city was proud of them for they had added another brilliant jewel to its crown and honour and another splendid page to its history of glorious tradition. The Bishop also spoke a few words of welcome, and to the strains of the 'Lincolnshire Poacher' the procession to the barracks then commenced: only two hundred yards had been covered when the gentlemen in khaki were in the arms of their wives and sweethearts, and the crowd and the soldiers got inextricably mixed, everyone wishing to shake the hands with the returning heroes.

Of the 133 Volunteers who left Lincolnshire at the country's call only 85 on Thursday returned. Disease had been rampant and seven at least died of enteric ... Lance Corporal Barker of Grantham was killed at Nitral's Nek. Many others had been invalided home whilst several are still in hospital at Pretoria.

The Volunteers, too, have had their full share of fighting, and were amongst the first to come in sight of Pretoria. Their grit, however, was particularly shown at Nitral's Nek, when Sergeant Rawdin worked the Maxim which practically saved the D and E Companies. When it jambed under fire he dissected it and recoupled it, his conduct being described by Mr Bennett Burleigh, the war correspondent, as amongst the most heroic witnessed during the campaign. When at length, almost surrounded by the enemy, he attached the ropes, and then eight of the Lincolnshire Volunteers who had remained under cover a short distance away, ran out and pulled the bullet-pitted gun in safety. This is but one of the Lincolnshire Volunteers' doings, and it is no wonder that the country is proud of the men who have so upheld its honour and its fame.

Celebrations took place at all the towns listed. In addition to Walter's home town of Scunthorpe, two, Brigg and Grimsby, have been selected as typical of the festivities around the region.

BRIGG

HOME SWEET HOME

A most enthusiastic reception was accorded the Brigg volunteers (Privates H. Sergeant and G. Peck) on their return on Saturday. The town was not lavishly decorated but the weather was delightful. Long before the arrival of the train the approaches to the station were crowded. The Volunteers, under the command of Col. Sergeant Knight, and headed by the Wrawby Prize Band, marched to the station. When the heroes of the hour left the train the band struck up with 'Home Sweet Home', which was followed with rounds of cheering and a rush was made to shake hands with the warriors in khaki. The men were then escorted to their homes, the band playing lively airs and followed by a large concourse of people. Col. Sgt Knight spoke a few words of welcome and Sergeant Johnson responded. The men, with the other Volunteers, and accompanied by the band, attended the morning service at the Parish Church, and an appropriate sermon was preached by the Vicar.

ADDRESS OF WELCOME

Delightful weather prevailed for the demonstration which took place on Wednesday afternoon. Shortly before the appointed time a large crowd assembled in the Market Place. The Volunteers, the returned Volunteers and Reservists, accompanied by the Church Lads Brigade were drawn up in front of the Town Hall, and after the Wrawby Prize Band had played a selection, the chairman of the Council, Mr J. Spring, said although there were serious differences as to the war waging in

South Africa,[13] *the inhabitants of Brigg were united in desiring to express their gladness on the safe return of the Volunteers and in giving them a hearty welcome. The policy of the war was with the statesmen and not with the soldiers, whose duty it was to respond to the call of duty. The country recognised the ready response given by the Volunteers and whilst they had been away their prayer had been that they might have a safe return. They also acknowledged the sacrifices the Volunteers had made and were most glad to see them safe home again from the dangers to which they had been exposed. They deeply regretted the illness of that gallant officer – Captain Stephenson – and their hearts went out to him in his sickness. Their prayers were that Providence would watch over him and speedily restore him to health.*

[The returning Volunteers were asked to accept the following address.] *On behalf of the citizens of Brigg we, as their elected representatives, beg to tender you a most hearty welcome and desire to express our sincere thankfulness at having you amongst us again.*

We cannot but remember that, at a time when the prospects of the War were unfavourable to our country, and our Colony was invaded by our enemy, you came forward and of your own free will volunteered to leave your homes and face the horrors and dangers of war in order to defend your countrymen in South Africa and to uphold the honour of our flag.

We, who have lived at home in ease and comfort, cannot properly realise the sacrifices you have cheerfully encountered in obeying the call of duty, but we can and do recognise the brave and loyal spirit which animated your action.

This war, terrible though it has been in many ways, has shown the world that the old spirit is not dead which enabled Britain in the past to plant the glorious flag of freedom in all quarters of the globe and that Britain's sons today from all quarters of the Empire will aid in maintaining that flag and the liberty that flourishes under it.

On behalf of our town we thank you for your noble response to the call of our country in her hour of need. We, your friends and townsmen, are proud of you and our hearts beat high with pride and gratification when we remember that our little Town has sent some of its Citizens to uphold the honour of our beloved country and the Town of Brigg.

[At a dinner given in their honour] *Mr F.C. Hett ... said that he little thought ten years ago when he assisted ... in forming the Volunteer contingent in Brigg that he should have the honour of proposing that glorious toast on an occasion like that. Volunteers were then, he feared, regarded as playing at soldiers. Now there was an entire change as to that assertion. Volunteers from England, Scotland, Ireland, Wales, India, South Africa, Canada, New Zealand and Australia have come forward and assisted the regular army in the war in which the country has been plunged.*

A war like the present had never occurred in the olden times when the army could see its foes. In South Africa the men knew practically nothing of the enemy, except the bullets whistling and comrades falling around them. It seemed to him in present warfare the men needed great nerve. The men must have gone through a terrible experience in having the enemies shooting at them from behind kopjes and trenches. Mr Hett touchingly referred to the dark days in 1899 and the sad disasters that befell British Arms in South Africa. But the Imperial Forces had shown the resources of a united Empire in such a manner as astonished the world. The men had proved themselves to be composed of men whom Lord Roberts had characterised as heroes on the battlefield and gentlemen at all other times. He congratulated Brigg for the Volunteers who left their homes to fight for their country.

GRIMSBY'S WELCOME

The anniversary of the relief of Mafeking was celebrated at Grimsby on Saturday in a notable and enthusiastic manner, for on that day nine of the volunteers from the ranks of the Rifles, being disbanded at Lincoln, arrived home, after being in South Africa since February of last year. The town was not so lavishly decorated. The enthusiasm was great. Being favoured with delightful weather, people flocked early to the Town Hall Square to have a good view of the procession from there to the Town Station to meet the heroes of the day. About 2.30 everything was in readiness and a start made ...

The procession marched to the Town Station. All along the route dense crowds has assembled and almost all the windows of the houses were occupied. Arriving at the station yard, the Rifles drew up two abreast to allow the civic authorities to pass through onto the station. Punctually to time the train steamed into the station, a number of fog signals on the line heralding its approach. As the bronzed faces and khaki helmets of the men were seen, the whole crowd on the station

136

sent up ringing cheers and a rush was made for the special compartment in which they were seated. When the train had stopped there was a mighty rush of friends and relations to grasp the hands of the brave volunteers, the first to welcome them being the borough member, who had succeeded in planting himself immediately in front of the carriage in which they travelled. Everyone of the nine men looked in the pink of condition although their khaki uniforms and kit gave evidence of pretty hard usage. The men, amidst wild cheering, marched out of the station and took up their position behind their old bugle band ...

In the Town Hall Square the scene was an animated one. In front and on either side, and straight down the street, there was a huge crowd of people, who eagerly watched the procession as it reached the civic building, and cheered in downright English fashion. A guard of honour was then formed by the Rifles and the men were taken into the Town Hall and on the balcony where they were welcomed by the Ex-mayor, Alderman Doughty M.P.

SCUNTHORPE

A GRAND WELCOME

Scunthorpe excelled itself on Saturday in giving such a magnificent welcome to its citizens who have proved themselves to be indeed worthy Sons of the Empire. We have had a few demonstrations the last of which 'Mafeking' was a fine outburst of genuine enthusiasm evoked by the noble deeds and self-sacrifice of British soldiers and it was peculiarly fitting that just 12 months after Mafeking relief should come home to friends and kindred the first active service Volunteers sent from Scunthorpe after some 15 months endurance of all toils and hardships and glories of war. Alas for the tinge of sadness that creeps in when we think of Private Skinner – one of the finest soldiers of the band that went out – and who fell victim to the dread enteric and was buried in far-off Bloemfontein. Lance Corporal Hockney arrived home some short time ago, he having been invalided, and now the five remaining whose time of Active Service has expired are homecoming. Privates Alex Charlesworth, W.S. Barley, J.W. Drury, T. Rhodes and W. Marris.

Scunthorpe is in a joyous, festive humour. The decorations are pretty and effective especially as we pass through High Street and

137

along Frodingham Road. The motto 'Welcome Home' is very much in evidence, but the Constitutional Club carried off the palm for a pretty show. The motto over the balcony says, 'Success To Our Army', the windows are set off with pretty rosettes of various hues, and flags and streamers fly all round and across the road. At night the fairy lamps are lit and the King's Coat of Arms appears ...

At the railway station long before six o'clock – the hour when the heroes are to arrive – thousands of people line the roadways and every approach is crowded. Even the hoardings are taken advantage of by the venturesome ones, and the railway bridge over the line is simply packed with people. Only a favoured few can be accommodated on the platform ...

The G and H Companies 3rd Vol. Battalion Lincolnshire Regiment, muster in good force commanded by their popular officer, Captain G.V. Dove. The Boys Brigade under Captain W.C. Thompson ... and a pleasing feature is a company of little girls representing the Red Cross in [the] *charge of Miss Nansen, headmistress of the Girls' National School, and these take collections on the way in aid of the Soldiers and Sailors Families Association. Supt. Marshall is in charge of the police but the crowd is a very orderly one and does not give much trouble.*

The train is up to time and the cracking of fog signals bespeaks the approach of the men Scunthorpe delights to honour. The first to be pulled out of the carriage is Charlesworth and he is quickly followed by the others, and the scene that follows is better felt than described. Amidst the shouts and the congratulations of many friends, the men are conducted to a waggonette where Mr Fletcher, Mr Woodley, Sergeant W. Gibson, the honorary secretary of the Reception Committee, have already taken their places and the men are joined by Lance Corporal Hockney.

When order has been restored somewhat, Mr Fletcher, on behalf of the townspeople of Frodingham and Scunthorpe District, and in a clear and distinct voice heard by many but not all standing around.

He said, 'Volunteers in your country's service, we meet you here today to greet you with a hearty welcome on your safe return from the seat of war. We welcome you on behalf of your friends and comrades. We welcome you on behalf of the inhabitants of this district, who would honour you for the gallant service you have rendered to your country. Fifteen months ago, full of zeal and patriotism, you volunteered to give up homes and friends, to sacrifice, if need be, even life itself in your country's service.

'You went away with the best wishes and earnest prayers of many friends that you might prove true and valiant soldiers; that in the heat of battle the kind hand of Providence might guide and protect you, and at the completion of your term of service, bring you back to home and friends in safety. Many have watched for news day by day as it arrived from the seat of war, anxious to know how it fared with the men who volunteered from this district. When you left us we little realised the desperate undertaking you had entered upon. We can, in some degree, understand the courage and endurance required for active service, but we fear we have little conception of the privations and hardship and the severe strain upon your courage and endurance in the conflicts through which you have been called to pass during the past 15 months. We rejoice with you and thank God for your safe return. Our rejoicing today is tinged with sadness. Some hearts mourn a loss. We miss in our midst a face and form once familiar to many here. We think of one who went out with you full of life and hope. Poor Skinner died in the service of his country; he fell victim to the dreadful disease which has laid low so many brave sons of the Empire. You have left him lying with many comrades in that distant land but his memory will linger with us still.

'Your friends will be anxious at this time to show you kindness. If I may be allowed to offer a word of counsel, I would do it by calling to the attention of each and all the desire of your great Commander-in-Chief expressed in the manifesto he has on your behalf issued to the British Public, signed ROBERTS.

'It will soon be your lot to enter again upon the ordinary duties of life. May the courage you have displayed in battle be yours to combat and conquer every temptation and every difficulty which may cross your path in the future. May you long live to be honoured and esteemed in this district for your courage and integrity. We hope that day is not far distant when we shall welcome home your comrades now serving at the front. When the time arrives and this war is over, we trust a generous public will raise in our district a permanent memorial to commemorate the fact that you and your comrades now on active service went out as Volunteers in your country's service – Barley, Charlesworth, Drury, Hockney, Marris, Rhodes, on behalf of your friends and comrades and this vast concourse of people, we give to each and all a hearty welcome home.'

The bands of the Rifles, Christian Temperance and the Boys' Brigade struck up lively airs and the huge procession wended its way to Scunthorpe where at the Parish Church a public Thanksgiving Service was held ... After service the procession reformed round the town *through some of the principal streets to the Drill Hall where the men were dismissed to their homes and friends.*

Private Marris was escorted by the Rifles Band to his home in Brumby where he had another welcome home all for himself.

BANQUETS AND SPEECHES

The six active service Volunteers just returned from the front ... were entertained to a half crown dinner by Mr Walter Crooke, engineer of the Frodingham Steel Works, in the Assembly Room on Wednesday night. Mr Crooke kindly entertained the men before they went out and now had the pleasure of repeating his generosity. On this occasion alas! there was one less to be treated viz. Private F. Skinner, who was one of the finest and liveliest of the company on the previous occasion. The Reservists were not forgotten on Wednesday night. Councillor Fletcher J.P. kindly undertook the footing of their bill. There were four Reservists who have been actively engaged in South Africa and these were Privates Unwin and W. Skelton, 2nd Coldstreams, Tidswell of the Border Regiment and Turner of the Yorks and Lancaster Regiment ...

Mr J. Fletcher J.P. [proposed] the toast to the gallant men of the Army and Navy who formed the defensive forces of the Empire. He trusted they would never be the first to throw down a challenge for war and so become the offensive forces. The history of England was full of splendid achievements, both on sea and land. Those who had followed the doings of the soldiers and sailors recently would acknowledge that the men of today were equal to the men of the past. (Cheers) He could imagine the Reservists had no idea of being called upon for active service, but to their credit, be it said, they were ready when the call came. (Cheers) He wished to say how proud they were of the men who returned on Saturday night last, and he thought the crowd who turned out to greet them was the largest he had ever seen in the neighbourhood. The Volunteers had worthily upheld the traditions of the British Army and had set an example for others to follow ...

Mr Walter Crooke proposed 'The Active Service Volunteers and Guests of the Evening'. He had the greatest pleasure in meeting them safe home again and they owed them a great debt for the service they had rendered. Whilst the officers had been severely criticised by foreigners and those at home,[14] all had praise for the soldiers who had served their country so nobly. They owed them a debt which they would never be able to repay. (Cheers) The toast was drunk with musical honours.

*Private Barley responded in a few words, and then Colour Sergeant
Fowler read an interesting account of the work of the Lincolns in South
Africa.*

*The Chairman, in presenting each of the men with a gold pendant
and a silver-mounted cane – the latter being the gift of Sgt. Major
Newberry, and the gold pendant presented by the Reception Committee
– said they could give them no recompense for what they had done but
they were asked to accept a small acknowledgement, not for the
intrinsic worth of the gifts but as a small token of their heartfelt
gratitude. The gold pendants bore the inscription –*

*'1st Battalion Lincolnshire Regiment, K Company, presented to Private
—— on his return from active service in South Africa 1901.'*

Alas, when his letters came to light nearly 85 years later, there was no sign of either
the pendant or the cane presented to Walter Barley.

The most poignant memories of that exciting time were held by his favourite
niece, May, who, although only just four years old, remembered vividly the excitement of the day of return and the crowds surrounding the house trying to get a
glimpse of the returned hero through the lace curtains. May, being so young at the
time, was not able to remember whether Uncle Walter took to heart Lord Roberts'
plea on the consumption of alcohol!

A family photograph of the period (Fig. 9) shows Walter, in civilian clothes
and holding in his arms his youngest niece, Molly, standing outside the back of his
home with his mother, Eliza, his sister Lillie and the two oldest nieces, Lenna and
Ada. May, for whatever reason, was not present for this photograph. As there is
snow on the ground, it was probably taken when the family moved from Sheffield
to Scunthorpe some months after Walter's return.

MEANWHILE …

While the Lincolnshire Volunteers waited for demobilisation and then made their
way home, skirmishes with the Boer commandos, such as the one in which
Walter's company had been involved, continued. In February 1901, Kitchener,
convinced that the time was ripe for a settlement, proposed peace talks to take
place at Middelburg. A ten-point plan was to be offered to Botha, but Alfred
Milner, equally convinced that the Boers should be conclusively defeated, was

Fig. 9 Walter with his mother, Eliza, his sister Lillie and three of his nieces, from the left, Ada, Molly and Lenna, in the garden of 29 Winterton Road, late 1901.

strongly against the move. He insisted on vetting the offered terms, and the British Government, when consulted, rejected two of them – those relating to an amnesty for 'colonial rebels' and to limited franchise rights for Africans.

Botha's rejection of the terms did not reach Kitchener until early May and, in the meantime, he stepped up the drives not only against the guerrillas but against the whole Boer population on the grounds that they harboured and supplied the commandos. Huge 'refuges', soon to be renamed 'concentration camps', were set up for the Boer civilians. Little thought was given to health and safety and the death toll, as a result of poor and inadequate food, lack of medical care and epidemics such as the enteric diseases and measles to which those from isolated farms had little immunity, rose to alarming proportions.[15]

Emily Hobhouse, who had visited many of the camps early in 1901, returned to Britain in May and intensified her campaign against the policy.[16] The British Government was eventually forced to act and sent out a House of Commons Commission, the 'Ladies Commission', headed by the suffragist Millicent Fawcett, to assess and report on conditions and to suggest remedies. Emily Hobhouse was not impressed and dubbed it the 'Whitewash Commission'.[17]

The Commissioners arrived in South Africa at the end of August 1901 and presented their report in December. They were joined by other women in South Africa, notably the Cape Town doctor Jane Waterston, and visited most of the camps. Their report criticised many aspects of the running of the camps, and their recommendations led to a considerable amelioration of conditions. By early 1902, hospitals and schools, staffed by nurses and teachers recruited mainly from Britain and Canada, had been set up.[18] At the end of the war, when the camps were disbanded, many of the teachers stayed on to help re-establish education in the Transvaal and the Orange River Colony. Some, in twos, trekked with the families to their home areas and set up farm schools for the Boer children.[19]

Notes to Part Two

As far as modern typography allows, all the letters are reproduced exactly – warts and all – from the MSS. News extracts are also quoted faithfully from the originals, except in so far as certain typographic features – notably the erratic use of quotation marks – are silently regularised. Authorial interpolations appear within brackets.

1. Kipling's verses are reproduced by kind permission of A.P. Watt Ltd. on behalf of the National Trust for Places of Historic Interest or Natural Beauty. All extracts are quoted from C. Carrington (ed.), *The Complete Barrack-Room Ballads of Rudyard Kipling*, London, 1973, Part 3 – Service Songs.
2. Unless otherwise stated, the details of the military campaigns are taken from T. Pakenham, *The Boer War*, Illustrated Edition, London, 1993. This edition, abridged by Toby Buchan, omits some of the painstaking details of the 1979 version but follows the sequence of events with great clarity.
3. See Appendix 2: the texts of Lord Roberts's Proclamations of March 1900.
4. D. Reitz, *Commando: A Boer Journal of the Boer War*, London, 1929, p. 161.
5. Pakenham 1979, p. 547.
6. Reitz in *Commando*, p. 247, claims that the only reason for taking uniforms was the need for clothing. He does not, however, explain why the commandos did not remove British badges etc.
7. Amery and Williams (eds), *The Times History of the War in South Africa*, Vol. 4, p. 249.
8. For details of offers made to serving soldiers to stay in South Africa see M. Streak, *Lord Milner's Immigration Policy for the Transvaal 1899–1905*, Johannesburg, 1969, p. 69.
9. Swaisland, *Servants and Gentlewomen*, pp. 154-5.
10. 'Slim' – Afrikaans meaning sly, cunning or clever.
11. A reference to the 'Khaki Election' of October 1900. See Pakenham 1993, p. 338.
12. 'Sjambok' – Afrikaans, a stout rhinoceros or hippopotamus hide whip.
13. It would be interesting to know what 'serious differences' were being referred to. It may be assumed that concentration camps and soldiers' health were two issues.

14. Criticisms of officers appear in the letters but one of the most damning accounts appears in (R. Rankin), *A Subaltern's Letters to His Wife*, London, 1901, in his chapter on 'Army Reorganisation', pp. 57–85. Rankin is not named as the author but Price identifies him in a footnote: *An Imperial War*, p. 179.

15. For a full discussion of the establishment of the camps and conditions therein, see A.C. Martin, *The Concentration Camps: Facts, Figures and Fables*, Cape Town, 1957.

16. Pakenham 1993, p. 252.

17. An account of the Ladies Commission and its work may be found in R. Strachey, *Millicent Garrett Fawcett*, London, 1931, pp. 190–200.

18. Swaisland, pp. 137-9, on the recruitment and role of teachers and nurses for the camps. The letters of Lilian Rose, a teacher recruited in Britain, who served in Burgher Camp, Natal, are housed in the Killie Campbell Library, Durban; see also Swaisland, p. 138.

19. Referred to in Sir Fabian Ware, 'The Milner Papers', in *Nineteenth Century*, Vol. 114, November 1933, p. 638.

PART THREE

Conclusions

Chapter 11

The Last Year of the South African War

May 1901 to May 1902

After Botha's rejection of the Middelburg peace terms and the stepping up of drives against the commandos, Kitchener decided that a new strategy was called for. A series of blockhouses was to be built, in close proximity to one another and linked together by barbed wire.[1] These would follow and protect the railway lines and criss-cross the Transvaal, the renamed Orange River Colony and the borders with Cape Colony. Their purpose would be to contain the commandos and make them easier to capture as well as to prevent them from invading Natal and the Cape. It was a massive task that would take many months to complete.[2]

The British Cabinet, meanwhile, was becoming increasingly alarmed by the mounting cost of the war and wished not only to bring it to a speedy end but to cut costs by reducing the size of the army in South Africa. Kitchener was against any such reduction, believing that the Boers still had the will and resources to carry on the conflict for many months. He feared a rebellion among the Afrikaners of Cape Colony and advocated severe measures against any who should carry or take up arms against the British. Any commandos found wearing British uniform were to be summarily executed. Although these orders were somewhat toned down at the insistence of the British Cabinet, fifty-one of those captured in British uniform were executed.

The Boers, meanwhile, were placing their hopes on uprisings in Cape Colony and Natal which would make possible an invasion by the commandos from the north. To this end, General P.H. Kritzinger and Judge Hertzog moved into the Cape early in 1901. Although this move failed, the idea was not abandoned. In September, a small commando led by General Jan Smuts succeeded in crossing the Orange River through the line of blockhouses defending it. The terrible hardships suffered by both men and their mounts has been graphically described by Deneys Reitz in his book *Commando*.[3] They had one great success when, on 17 September, the commando decisively defeated the 11th Lancers at Elands River Poort. The fresh mounts, guns and ammunition captured enabled them to continue far longer than would otherwise have been possible, although their efforts had little effect on the outcome of the war. The clothing, mainly British uniforms captured on this occasion, led to many of them being summarily shot as spies.[4]

In the same month, Botha crossed the Buffalo River into Natal and other small commandos penetrated the British lines and entered the Cape. These incursions, despite some successes, proved to be forlorn hopes. Botha's commando, after an abortive attack on two British forts on the borders of Zululand, was forced to make a hasty retreat into the Transvaal. Smuts and the other commandos were left isolated in remote parts of the Cape and soon accepted that there would be no uprising of the Cape Afrikaners. The hope of creating a spearhead for an invasion of the Cape by De la Rey and a large Transvaal army had to be abandoned.

By the end of the year the construction of the blockhouse lines was nearing completion, and protected areas around Bloemfontein and the Rand had been set up from which British drives could work outwards to clear the country of guerrillas. Each month the number of Boers captured increased until most of the central areas were clear. However, in the north-east corner of the Orange River Colony, Steyn and De Wet still held out, as did De la Rey in the west of the Transvaal and Botha in the east. By December 1901 De Wet was desperately short of supplies and mounts but decided to launch a concentrated attack on the uncompleted eastern arm of the defence line running from Kroonstad towards the Natal border. Early on Christmas morning he attacked the Yeomanry camp at Tweefontein and caught them unawares.[5] Quantities of supplies and armaments were captured and some prisoners taken, but these were only held long enough to relieve them of their clothes before they were freed to return to their camps.

The blockhouse system was completed by early February and a series of massive drives was set in train. Four British columns attempted to trap De Wet and Steyn against the lines, but the two most wanted Boer leaders managed to find a weak link in the defences and slip through. A second drive was more successful, capturing General Lucas Meyer's commando of nearly eight hundred men as well as cattle, horses and wagons. In early March, Steyn and De Wet again evaded capture by slipping through the lines. They joined up with De la Rey who had recently achieved his own victory over the British at Tweebosch.

Kitchener was dismayed by the failure to capture the leaders, but the commandos were now in such a poor state, lacking equipment and mounts, that they were unable to profit from their successes. The end of the conflict was in sight. The last formal battle of the war took place at Rooiwal on 11 April, when Generals Kemp and Potgieter attacked a large British force with an ill-advised cavalry charge. Potgieter was killed and many of the Boers managed to escape only because the British did not follow up their advantage. On the same day, a Boer delegation left for Pretoria to begin negotiations for a settlement.

The peace talks began in earnest on 15 May when sixty Boer delegates, elected from the commandos, met at Vereeniging south of Pretoria. The deliberations were long and bitter with disagreements on both sides. On the British side there was dissension between Kitchener, who wanted to end the war, and Milner, who still believed that too much was being offered to the Boers. The British Government, after much debate, sided with Kitchener. On the Boer side there were divisions between the 'Bitter Enders', such as Steyn and De Wet, who believed there was still a chance of victory, and those among the Transvaalers who knew that they no longer had the resources to carry on.

A major factor that had brought the Afrikaners to the negotiating table was their awareness of the terrible suffering and distress of the women and children who, by Kitchener's orders of December 1901, had been denied entry to the camps and were roaming the veld without means of support. Kitchener had ordered this change of policy in the belief that having to care for their families would handicap the commandos in their guerrilla operations and, therefore, would bring them more rapidly to the conference table.[6]

A vote on 31 May 1902 of the Boer delegates was passed, by fifty-four to six, in favour of accepting the peace terms. The signing of the surrender terms took place at Pretoria the same evening. The long war was at an end.

Creating the peace was yet to begin.

Chapter 12

What the Documents Reveal

INTRODUCTION

The letters of Walter Barley and his companions add little to knowledge of the events and strategy of the South African War, but they reveal much of the experiences, conditions and feelings of the men at the bottom of the British military hierarchy. Supporting documents from the Lincolnshire press provide valuable evidence of what was available to family and friends for moulding their opinions on the war as well as building up a picture of the day-to-day lives of their menfolk in South Africa. One can only surmise, however, on the accuracy of these impressions when filtered through the limited experience of the families left behind.

The letters are particularly useful in that they were written by men who, although low in the hierarchy, were more articulate than most of the private soldiers of the Regular Army. Many of the Volunteers had accepted a lowering of social status by offering themselves for service as private soldiers. This is commented upon not only by those who knew them in their home surroundings but also by the Volunteers themselves. Sergeant Hancock of the East Yorkshire Volunteers, for instance, remarked that 'the change between the living of a fairly well-to-do civilian and a soldier with the Field Force is great indeed'.

The letters often appear to reflect a limited view of the nature and extent of the events in which the Volunteers were involved. This may be due more to the circumstances of service, which frequently isolated the serving soldier from major events, than, in the case of the Volunteers, to any lack of education. Soldiers may also have restricted their letter-writing to topics that they felt would interest the recipients. Walter, in writing to his mother and sisters, may have assumed that a discussion of war strategy would have been of less interest than details of his day-to-day life. In the days before extensive media coverage by radio and television, there are few ways of knowing what the men discussed around the campfire or among themselves when no one else was listening. The letters may, therefore, present a restricted account of the full experience and perceptions of the men at the front. The presence among Walter's papers of the copy of the Bloemfontein *Friend*, and his comment from Tulbagh that newspapers came up from Cape Town, indicates that he had some access to local news which would have kept him in touch with military developments.

It is possible that, when experiencing shortages of food and other supplies, soldiers attributed some of their difficulties to the wrong causes. The men often complained, for example, that the shortages were due to neglect by the War Office. While there was undoubtedly an element of truth in this, such shortages were often caused by the great distances over which supplies had to be transported as well as by the capture of supply columns by the Boers. The priorities of those at the top of the military hierarchy may also have had the effect of depriving the lower ranks of what they regarded as their due. Lord Roberts, for example, was known to be irritated by the slowness of the supply columns and, perhaps unintentionally, to sacrifice the welfare of the men to what he regarded as the necessary speed of advance. Whatever the reasons, there is no doubt that at times the efficiency of the British Army was impaired by lack of supplies. The health of the men suffered from shortages of water and food, and the high rate of illness was the result, in part at least, of the privations they suffered. The lack of adequate and appropriate clothing and bedding also had an effect on health and no doubt on morale. On occasions soldiers were even prevented by these lacks from playing their parts in military engagements.

The privations suffered by those who volunteered for service so enthusiastically at the beginning of the war inevitably changed their views of it. Why did they rush so eagerly to enlist? There was certainly an element of adventure-seeking, particularly in view of the restricted lives and the hardships which were the lot of the British working class of the time.[7] The build-up of an atmosphere of jingoism in the later nineteenth century also provided a powerful incentive.[8] The massive emigration movement to all parts of the Empire was built not only on economic necessity but also on the strong belief that the dissemination of Anglo-Saxon culture and the Christian faith was a duty laid on those privileged to have inherited them.[9] These beliefs may not have been as clear to those who volunteered for service as to the missionaries and administrators whose work was to put them into practice, but the perceived challenge to this ethos by a small band of backveld farmers may have stirred up latent feelings of imperial pride and duty.[10]

What is clear is that the euphoria of the early months of the war, with its urgent demand for enlistment, was not maintained. An important reason for this was undoubtedly an economic one. The outbreak of the South African War followed years of one of the deepest economic recessions of the modern era, and unemployment has always provided a strong incentive to enlistment in the Regular Army. As the general economic situation improved during the war years, in part at least because of the war, the rush to enlist decreased dramatically.[11]

The Volunteer Movement was not affected to the same extent by economic considerations as its members came from a rather higher and more secure social stratum than those who took 'the Queen's shilling'.[12] In their case, it is clear that the strongest incentive was a search for adventure, a taste for which had been engendered by the activities of the Volunteers at their parades, competitions and camps. In their case, too, the number of volunteers decreased as the war advanced but not to the same extent as for the Regular Army.[13]

Walter Barley writes little about his motives for volunteering as these would have been well known to his family and friends in Scunthorpe. He expresses the same wish to put the Boers in their place as many others. He did, however, as the war dragged on, express increasingly frequently his wish to be back in England enjoying the activities of his Volunteer comrades left at home. He was quite adamant that he did not wish to take up any offer of employment in South Africa as he liked England better.

THE HEALTH OF THE COMMON SOLDIER

A major preoccupation in all the letters is the physical state of the men. This must, of course, be viewed in the context of the medical knowledge and health practices of the day. Walter commented constantly on the way he treated himself for ailments, real or imagined. Much of his preoccupation was with the state of his bowels and he followed the general precept of the day that 'inner cleanliness' solved most of the problems of the body. Soon after arrival in South Africa he wrote of his relief that he could buy 'salts' for this purpose. The local beer, he said, 'binds me instead of working me'. When he was unable to purchase salts he took soap pills as an alternative. Later, while on guard duty on the hills north of Pretoria, he took a Beecham's Pill every day and was convinced that that was why he never succumbed to the dreaded enteric fever.

Before the development of antibiotics half a century later, ailments which would now be regarded as relatively minor were often life-threatening. Several of the Volunteers on the transport *Guelph*, on the voyage to South Africa, fell ill and one at least died of what Walter believed to be pneumonia, although he attributed the cause to 'sitting on the deck at sunset when the change comes in the wind'. He added, however, that the health of the men seemed to be 'worse without oranges and apples'. Low levels of vitamin C were known as a factor contributing to poor health at sea, but this voyage was hardly long enough for such deficiencies to develop. The crowded conditions below decks, with the inevitable spread of infection, was the more likely cause of poor health.

While Walter's company was in Cape Province, within reach of regular supplies from the coast as well as fresh vegetables and fruit from the immediate area, health was good. The men even supplemented their diet with fresh fish, caught in the local streams. Walter commented that they had never enjoyed better health, and Hockney added that the country agreed with them. Walter thought their good health was due to the bathes they took every morning.

Later, when on the march and separated from regular supplies, diarrhoea and dysentery became serious problems. Walter never complained of them but others of his group suffered so badly that they were hospitalised. The quality of the water they were forced to drink probably accounted for such outbreaks as well as for the much more serious enteric fever from which so many soldiers died, including Fred Skinner of Walter's company. Walter complained of the unsavoury quality of the drinking water that they were, at times, obliged to take from rivers and pools. He wrote that the men drank any sort of water, 'dead horses and mules in it or else go without'. An unnamed commentator on the same march was particularly incensed that the officers used the water from the water-carts for baths and 'Tommy has to go two miles if he wants any'. Walter recalled in a later letter that on the long march their Colonel had used 'two or three buckets of good water to bath himself', while they were dying for a drink and not able to wash for a week. Marris reported to his parents that, after one march, they were each given half a can of muddy water that had to be boiled before drinking to avoid infection.

Although far more men suffered from illness than wounds, the after-effects of being wounded in battle could be very serious in view of the great distances to be covered to get the men to hospital and the shortage of medical supplies when they got there. Many were stabilised at the scene and then transported to the nearest hospital by horse-drawn ambulance. If they survived but were unfit for further service, they were taken to the coast by hospital train and repatriated. Traces of ambivalence can be detected in the letters in relation to wounding or other injuries, due, no doubt, to the fact that, if the patient survived, he was either out of the fighting for some time or invalided home. Walter reported an incident when a bugler attempted to ride a horse bareback and was thrown onto rocks. He was picked up unconscious, 'so he is alright for a month or six weeks'.

One aspect of the men's health that has received relatively little attention is that of shell-shock. The condition was little understood in the South African War, or, indeed, in the First World War, when many men suffering from the condition were regarded either as malingerers or, even worse, as deserters for which execution was the penalty. In the South African War, the men were little prepared for the fury of battle. There had been no major conflict since the Crimean War so very few soldiers, even of the Regular Army, had experienced going into battle. They had left for South Africa believing that the Boers would be overcome without difficulty. No one, men or officers, was prepared for the guerrilla tactics employed by the Boer commandos who used surprise, ambush, accurate firing and knowledge of the terrain to compensate for small numbers and lack of formal military training. It is small wonder that, in the stress of battle often against an unseen enemy, particularly when the attack was sudden, the men could be demoralised to the point of breakdown.

The events of Black Week of December 1899 were particularly shocking to the troops on the ground, and to the British public as details of the British defeats filtered through. In Lincolnshire the horrifying details spread alarm and despondency. A letter in the *Lindsey and Lincolnshire Star* (3 February 1900, p. 2) from Sergeant Letts, regiment not stated, about the Battle of Magersfontein illustrates the point and the problem of shell-shock.

> *Our poor chaps were just mown down in hundreds. To make matters worse some 60 officers were shot down and then the men were completely demoralised, no-one to tell them where to go and what to do ... left as they were like sheep and all that day ... we kept meeting stragglers – some down in the open plains, fast asleep in the sun, others simply wandering aimlessly about and some, when they did eventually reach the baggage convoy, went raving mad and a couple of days afterwards, after the wounded had been sent to Cape Town, a big batch of lunatics had to be sent back under strong escort, some of them were so bad that I don't think they will ever recover their reason.*

One of the unthinkable outcomes of Black Week, and of subsequent defeats at the hands of the Boers, was the number of British soldiers taken prisoner. Many of these were taken to Pretoria and put into a camp on the racecourse. The Boers had even fewer supplies than the British and the result was that disease was rampant among the prisoners. On 28 April 1900 the *Lindsey and Lincolnshire Star* reported that the prisoners at Pretoria were in a deplorable state as the camp 'was unfit for humans and dangerous to health'. One hundred and eight of the men were suffering from dysentery, pneumonia and typhoid. There was no resident doctor and the water was black and muddy.

Walter, although spared the ravages of serious illness, complained of a series of minor ones. Whether these were real or imagined is difficult to tell. No doubt the trouble he had with his ears, which seriously impaired his hearing from time to time, was genuine. He first complained of it before leaving England when, while training at Grantham, he had a bout of 'influenza' which left him so deaf that he could not hear the orders given and was sent off duty. Walter believed that the only course of treatment was to have his ears syringed. As this produced no improvement, it is likely that he suffered from inflammation of the middle ear, otitis media. At one point he was relieved of guard duty on the hills above Pretoria after the Captain came up to him without being heard.

Walter was in hospital twice, once for a fortnight with an unspecified fever. Several times he reported trouble with his legs, either blistering after long marches or from 'twisting my knee a bit'. He spent several days in hospital with the latter. He does not, however, describe conditions in the hospitals or indicate whether they were army field hospitals or established local hospitals which had been taken over for war casualties.

Much has been written elsewhere about the hospitals of the South African War and the many British nurses who volunteered for service, many of whom died from the infections rife in them.[14] Private Hannah, who was shot through the chest at Nitral's Nek and spent time in several hospitals before reaching Cape Town for repatriation, spoke appreciatively of the care given and especially of the food in them.

CLOTHING AN ARMY

Walter and his companions left Britain well kitted out. Photographs of the day show him and his companions in both home and tropical kit. 'We have got all our Kharki suits', he reported from Grantham, adding that the local gentry and tradespeople had been very generous in providing them with items of clothing and other comforts, so that they had almost too many clothes and boots. This kit lasted well while the Volunteers were at Tulbagh, although with the heavy marching – 'since we have been here we have marched about 350 miles' – undertaken as part of the toughening-up process before moving up to the front line, their boots were soon in need of repair.

Walter claimed that his boots were the best in the company. Nearly all the others had to have theirs mended and he was going to buy a card of 'protectors' to keep his in good condition. The others had to march to a village four miles away to get them mended. The prices charged for repairs astonished him – 5s for two toecaps, 1s 6d for a patch on the heel and 8d for six protectors. Walter thought it was a bit much that they had to pay for repairs out of their own pockets. Considering that the daily pay of the men was 1s 3d and they had to pay not only for boot repairs but also for any food over and above the army rations, Walter's complaint is understandable.

After the march to Pretoria all the men were having problems with their kit. Marris wrote to his parents that they were all in tatters and badly shod but more was expected from Cape Town. When the Regiment was ordered out from Pretoria to meet Baden-Powell on the Rustenburg road, only ninety-five were able to march – 'the rest had bad boots and went sick when ordered on the march'. Walter was one who went sick on this occasion, but he appears to have been genuinely unwell.

It is obvious that the hoped-for supply of kit had not arrived by 11 July, when the Lincolns were involved in the engagement at Nitral's Nek. Walter was among the twenty-four unable to march because of the state of their boots. By this time, with the non-arrival of the new supply of clothing, the men were in a parlous state. The same correspondent that had complained of the use of the water-carts on the march to Pretoria described the state of men's clothes as they lined the streets for Lord Roberts to pass by. Their shirts were sticking out of the holes in their coats. His jacket was torn along the back, the back of his trousers was out and his knees were sticking through the legs.[15]

It was not until 23 August that Walter was able to report in a letter home that the new clothes had arrived from Cape Town. On 6 September he reported that they had been issued with new clothes – boots, shoes and socks – but he had only one shirt as there were not enough to go round and they had to draw lots for them. Welcome as was this issue of new kit, the relief did not last long. By early January Walter was complaining again of the state of his clothes. His company was on outpost near Rietfontein where it rained nearly every day and they were constantly wet through. Their clothes had to dry on them and he had only one shirt and that had not been washed for a month. Was this the same shirt that he had received in September? He was having to fasten his trousers together with string as they were falling to pieces.

The clothing situation was not helped by the fact that the Boers, when desperate for supplies of all kinds, did not hold captured British soldiers but released them after removing anything of use to the commandos – including, in some cases, their uniforms. This, it was claimed in an article in the *Hull Times*, had happened to 800 men taken prisoner by De Wet in Natal. They were put over the Natal border, having been robbed of their khaki uniforms, 'in the filthy clothes discarded by the Boers'.

The plight of the Mounted Infantry, the MI, when new supplies of clothing were not forthcoming, was also parlous. The *Lindsey and Lincolnshire Star* published an account on 29 September 1900 by N. Roberts, a Trooper in the Yorks Imperial, of the state of the men before the new issue arrived.

> *... to think that the British Government would allow us to go as we did in rags, riding forced marches of 28-30 miles a day with nothing*

but bare legs rubbing against the saddle. Until I got a pair of Cord pants off a Boer farm I was riding with one leg in my breeches and the other leg bare and I was not as bad as some of our fellows either – one or two had got no tunics, and our boots – some were walking in their bare feet. Two fellows in my troop ... had no soles at all just the tops left ... With getting this new rigout I am free from lice, thank heavens, for the first time since leaving Senekal ... You cannot wonder at us catching them when we are only allowed one blanket and carried under our saddle, they come off the horse into the blanket.

When Walter and his companions arrived home in May 1900 they were reported to be in good health 'but their khaki uniforms and kit gave evidence of pretty hard usage'.

FOOD FOR THE TROOPS

'An army marches on its stomach' has often been said, but both Walter and Marris wrote home about the shortage of food on the long march to Pretoria, complaining that they had been on half rations and even quarter rations – 'Fancy marching 25 miles in one day with nothing else only a biscuit and a bit'. Marris reported being on half rations for a week during the march, but at the Vaal River he was able to buy the best meal he had had in South Africa. He had bought 'a fowl hot out of the pot' from an African home he was guarding.

The situation improved once the Volunteers were on guard duty in Pretoria. They were able to buy extra supplies out of their own pockets as long as their money lasted. One meal often cost them a day's pay or more, as when Marris reported that they had bought boiled mutton and beans for 1s 6d. Walter wrote that they had been able to draw some of their pay, which they spent on food. They were no longer living on biscuits as they were issued with a pound of bread instead, which they ate at one meal. 'We have to buy some, we pay 6d a loaf, we often eat 3 a day so you can see what appetites we have.' Walter gave a list of the prices they had to pay for extra food and thought everything was very dear. A pound of jam, a tin of milk or salmon cost a day's pay, while a pound of butter or biscuits cost two days' pay. He sent a message to his sister Lillie telling her not to insult him 'about mackeral', when they were having dry bread and coffee for their evening meal. Later, as the Volunteers began to look forward to going home, Walter sent messages about the food he would like on his return, saying that in South Africa dry bread and jam and coffee was a 'spread fit for a king'. Cocoa was a great luxury, and he added that he had enjoyed many a good meal of 'sop', the Lincolnshire term for bread and milk.

Sergeant Hancock, in the letter published in the *Hull Times*, gave the most detailed and amusing account of the food available for the troops when far from lines of supply. The staple food was biscuit – 'patent dog biscuits' – out of which to make all their 'dainty dishes'. Four a day were allowed so they had to be careful not to eat a day's ration at one meal. He gave a list of the 'dainties' that could be made out of biscuit – gruel by smashing them very small and boiling them in water, or porridge by thickening them with more biscuit. He wrote an amusing and iron-ical account of making 'a nice suet pudding' out of the biscuits. To half a pint of mutton bone soup was added 'the shadow of a square of compressed vegetables'. They could not expect the vegetables to be in the soup as they had to be careful not to overload their stomachs and fall asleep on sentry duty, for which offence a soldier on active service could be liable to the penalty of death. Hancock described the special treat they had one day of a quarter-pound of jam per man. 'Didn't we have a royal time of it.' With such luxuries provided in such generous quantities, he wrote, they would never want to leave South Africa.

'Bully beef', tinned processed meat, was a staple of the men's diet, when there was any to be had. Hancock wrote that they understood the meaning of 'B and B' (bully and biscuit) but never saw any of the former. Walter, in the last weeks before demobilisation, when his company was on patrol near Rietfontein, wrote that although they were wet through every day, they did have plenty of bully beef, biscuits and jam. Private Maxwell, in his 'poetical description' of Christmas on the veldt, replied to the question as to whether the men had any Christmas fare, 'Not a particle'. For Christmas dinner, he told the reporter, they had nothing but bully beef, and for drink 'nothing liquid except a fond ... tear for those far away'.

Drink, other than the despised water, was usually coffee or tea. Beer, for which the men hankered, was in short supply, although they had been able to get plenty in the early weeks in South Africa. Walter wrote that he and Skinner had walked to the Yeomanry Camp twelve miles away and had been rewarded with a good tea with two buckets of beer among them all. The men had enjoyed a march to Ceres through the spectacular scenery of the Hex River Valley. They enjoyed it even more when the local magistrate, the Landdrost,[16] entertained them to tea in the park, with 'tea, biscuits and cheese, beer, stout and lemonade'. Walter wrote that, in Pretoria, although it was difficult to find beer, the men had had issues of rum. He was having a nice drink as he wrote the letter, having 'bought another ration for six pence'.

Towards the end of 1900, as the Volunteers waited for news of their demo-bilisation, Walter wrote that he was looking forward to a glass of Burton when he got home as it was over three months since they had had any beer. By this time he was resigned to the lack of it – 'I think we are teatotallers now'. It is not clear whether this was a spelling mistake or a bit of wry humour. He added philosoph-ically that they were better without it 'as it heats the blood'. As Christmas approached Walter began to order the beer he would like when he got home – a dozen bottles of Bass's beer to be bought as soon as they received his letter, so that they would be in good condition for his return. When Christmas came and they were still waiting for repatriation, he reported that they had been stood to arms on Christmas Day 'and no beer'.

Walter proved to be ingenious in adding to his spartan diet. When the Volunteers were on their final foray at Rietfontein before leaving for home, he took the opportunity of raiding the orchard at Joubert's Farm and having a good feed of peaches, apples, grapes, pomegranates, quinces and prickly pears. In a postscript to this letter he wrote that he had just been making some jam out of peaches and sugar.

Chapter 13

Epitaph for Walter Barley

> *But now, discharged, I fall away*
> *To do with little things again ...*
> *Gawd, 'oo knows all I cannot say,*
> *Look after me in Thamesfontein!*
>
> If England was what England seems,
> An' not the England of our dreams,
> But only putty, brass, an' paint,
> 'Ow quick we'd chuck 'er! *But she ain't!*
>
> Kipling – 'The Return'

It must have been difficult for Walter Barley to settle back into civilian and family life after his experiences on active service and the excitement of the return. No doubt he had the Volunteers and the Constitutional Club to add a little spice to a humdrum existence. He never married. May thought that he had once had a 'lady friend' in the years before he went to South Africa but she had married another. He seems never to have formed another attachment.

Walter settled back into his work as a painter and decorator. A photograph of about 1904 shows the family – his mother, Eliza; his sister Lillie; the four girls, Lenna, Ada, May and Molly – standing outside the house on Winterton Road (Fig. 10). On the wall above their heads is a board which proclaims –

W.S. BARLEY
PAINTER
PAPERHANGER &c

Fig. 10 Eliza Barley and the Stubbins family outside 29 Winterton Road, *c.* 1904; Walter Barley's signboard on the wall over their heads.

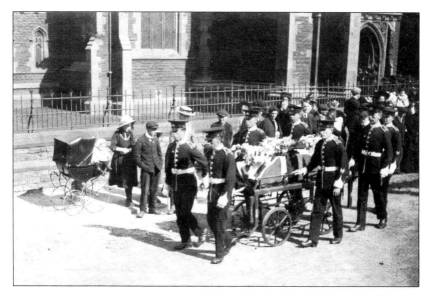

Fig. 11 Walter Barley's funeral, October 1910.

No doubt he painted it himself as May remembered that, when he was not out on decorating jobs, he worked in a shed in the back yard writing signboards and repainting and restoring the linework on prams.

Life must have changed when Lillie, Charlie and the girls moved from Sheffield to join Walter and his mother at 29 Winterton Road (see Fig. 9, p. 142). The house was large enough for them all with the little girls accommodated in the attic, but relationships, it seems, were often strained. Eliza was a forthright woman of whom the children were always a little afraid. Her son-in-law, Charlie, found it expedient to escape as often as possible when not at work. The 'publics' were readily available and this, along with the thirst engendered by his work in the steel industry as a 'fettler' charged with 'furnace wrecking', the term used for replacing the worn inner brick linings, led to a drink problem.[17] It did not improve relationships or the family finances. Lillie and the girls became ardent teetotallers and joined the Independent Order of Rechabites, a temperance society founded at Salford, Lancashire, in 1835.

There is no record of when Walter's health began to fail, but he died on 6 October 1910, at the age of forty years. Family tradition has it that he succumbed to a chest infection brought on by his war experiences of sleeping out on the veldt in the cold and wet. It is more likely that he suffered from the effects of chain-smoking exacerbated, perhaps, by the toxic fumes from the paints used at the time.

He may also have been tubercular, as were several members of the family. Molly, as a small child, suffered from tubercular glands in the neck, and carried the scars from the draconian home poulticing for the rest of her life. Ada was also tubercular and spent much of her childhood and adolescence in hospitals and sanatoria. My family, too, was affected. In 1930 my brother, then six years old, began to show ominous signs of tuberculosis. My father decided that the only course of action was to remove his children from the close contact with my mother's family and take us to the warmer climate of South Africa, then known as 'The Lungs of the Empire'. In the warmth of Cape Town and the clear air of Natal, where he attended the short-lived Quaker boarding school at Inchanga, my brother recovered his health.

Walter Barley was given a military funeral and escorted to the grave by his comrades in the Volunteers (Fig. 11). May mourned him deeply. Never since that day, she told me, had she been able to hear the 'Dead March from Saul' without being reduced to tears. She was always happy to talk about her beloved uncle, still green in her memory seventy years and more after his death.

Notes to Part Three

1. Pakenham 1993, p. 251, pp. 263–72, details the building and operation of the blockhouse system.
2. Walter mentions building a blockhouse earlier in the year (Letter 38). It was probably too early to be part of Kitchener's system, but it may be that Kitchener took the idea from some of the blockhouses already being built.
3. Reitz, *Commando*, pp. 199-309.
4. Ibid., p. 228.
5. The undated account by Private Maxwell, New South Wales Mounted Infantry, of Christmas on the veldt, although typical of any Christmas of the war, may refer specifically to the attack by De la Rey on the Yeomanry Camp at Tweefontein on 25 December 1901.
6. Pakenham 1979, p.548.
7. Price, *An Imperial War*, p.220 – on the search for adventure as a reason for enlistment.
8. Ibid., pp. 227–8.
9. This belief was strongly held by the women's emigration societies which facilitated the emigration of British women from the 1860s. It was held particularly strongly by the British Women's Emigration Association, which operated from 1884 to 1919.
10. Note the tone of the speeches made both before the departure of the Lincolnshire Volunteers and on their return.
11. Price, pp. 211-16 – on the relationship between the economic situation in Britain and enlistment.
12. 'Taking the Queen's, or King's, shilling' relates to an earlier practice of giving new recruits to the Regular Army a shilling when they were sworn in.
13. Price, *An Imperial War*, p. 214.
14. Swaisland, *Servants and Gentlewomen*, p. 153.
15. From the Scrapbook of the Lincolnshire Regiment in the Museum of Lincolnshire Life, Lincoln, dated 12 July 1900 but no evidence of source.
16. 'Landdrost' – Afrikaans – a magistrate with jurisdiction over a particular magisterial district or 'drostdy'. J. Branford, *Dictionary of South African English*, Cape Town, 1978.
17. See Creed and Coult, *Steeltown*: conditions inside the furnaces, p. 47; furnace wrecking with a mention of the gases found in the process, p. 71; thirst and the consumption of beer, pp. 75–7.

Appendix 1

ARMY ORDER NO. 1 – 1900

RULES FOR THE EMPLOYMENT OF AUXILIARIES

The conditions under which the services of the Volunteer forces will be accepted for duty in South Africa are thus stated in an Army Order issued by Lord Wolseley, Commander-in-Chief.

1. A carefully selected company of 116 of all ranks may be raised for each line battalion serving in, or about to proceed to, South Africa from the affiliated Volunteer battalions. This company will be attached for service to the line battalion in South Africa, and placed under the commanding officer of that battalion.
2. An equal number of waiting companies may be maintained at home.
3. The 5th (Irish) Volunteer Battalion Liverpool Regiment will furnish the company for the Royal Irish Regiment, and the 16th Middlesex (London Irish) for the Royal Irish Rifles.
4. The strength of each company will be:– One captain, two subalterns, one sergeant-instructor to act as pay sergeant, four sergeants, two buglers, five corporals, ninety-nine privates, and two stretcher-bearers; total of 116.
5. The selection of officers and the composition of each company will be controlled by the officer commanding the regimental district in which it is raised.

    In the case of line battalions having several affiliated Volunteer battalions, companies will be formed from about an equal number of men from each battalion, as the officer commanding the regimental district may decide.

    No Volunteer battalion will be allowed to contribute less than one complete section.
6. The following will be the qualifications for service:–
    a)   Every Volunteer must enlist for one year or for the war. In the event of the war being over in less than one year, he will have the option of being discharged at once or of completing his one year's service.
    b)   He must be not less than twenty nor more than thirty-five years of age.

c) He must be a first-class shot under Volunteer rules.

d) He must have been returned as efficient during 1898 and 1899.

e) He must be of good character.

f) He must be up to the physical standard of an infantry recruit as laid down in the Recruiting Regulations for the Army. No relaxation of standard will be allowed.

g) He must be medically fit for active service.

h) Preference should be given to unmarried men, or widowers without children. Married men should be accepted only in the event of an insufficient number of single men or widowers without children volunteering.

7. When a Volunteer commanding officer has received application from not less than a section of Volunteers, he will so inform the officer commanding the regimental depôt to which his battalion is affiliated, who will then, if they are to form part of the service company, have them medically inspected, and if fit for service, attested.

8. After attestation they will join the regimental depôt until required for embarkation. In the event of there not being sufficient barrack accommodation available, they may be billeted.

9. Volunteers accepted for the waiting companies will be attested, and passed to the reserve at once for the unexpired portion of their engagement, or until required for permanent service. During the time they are in the reserve they will receive reserve pay, and they will be liable to carry out the training laid down in the Reserve Forces Act, 1882.

10. General Officers Commanding will arrange for all Volunteers to receive, after enlistment, as much instruction in musketry, including range practice, as is possible prior to embarkation.

11. Every officer and man will be clothed and equipped under regimental arrangement exactly as those in the Regular battalion which they are to join, except that the numerals on the shoulder-cords will be as laid down in the Volunteer Regulations. For these purposes a special capitation of £9 will be granted to the corps for each Volunteer.

12. Each Volunteer will receive from date of enlistment pay and allowance of his rank as a regular infantry soldier, rations, and clothing. Should a married man be accepted, his family will be entitled to a separation allowance.

13. On completing his period of service he will receive a gratuity of £5, in addition to any gratuity given to the troops at the end of the war. If discharged in consequence of wounds, injuries, or disability received or contracted while on service, he will be entitled to pension in accordance with the Royal Warrant for Pay, etc., of the Regular Army.

14. On the departure of a company from the United Kingdom the officers and Volunteers composing it will be considered supernumerary to their corps.
15. Service in one of these companies will entitle an officer or Volunteer to be considered efficient for the year, and the corps will receive capitation grant accordingly for each Volunteer actually enlisted.

Quoted in full in Col. C.H. Hart, *First Volunteer Battalion of the Royal Warwickshire Regiment*, Midland Counties Herald Ltd, 1906, pp. 223–4.

Appendix 2

LORD ROBERTS'S PROCLAMATIONS, BLOEMFONTEIN, MARCH 1900

The following are taken from the tattered copy of *The Friend* found with Walter Barley's papers. It is addressed on the outside, in his handwriting, to The Secretary, Liberal Club, Scunthorpe, Lincolnshire, England, but may have been sent to his mother to be passed on. The words in brackets are indecipherable.

The Friend, No. 6, Bloemfontein, 24 March 1900, p. 1

PROCLAMATION
To the Burghers of the Orange Free State

The British troops under my command, having entered the Orange Free State, I feel it my duty to make known to all Burghers the cause of our coming, as well as to do all in my power to put an end to the devastation caused by this war, so that should they continue the war the inhabitants of the Orange Free State may not do so ignorantly, but with full knowledge of their responsibility before God for the lives lost in the campaign.

Before the war began the British Government, which had always desired and cultivated peace and friendship with the people of the Orange Free State, gave a [solemn promise] *to President Steyn that if the Orange Free State would remain neutral, the territory would not be invaded, and its independence would at all times be respected by Her Majesty's Government.*

In spite of that declaration, the Government of the Orange Free State was guilty of a wanton and unjustifiable invasion of British territory.

The British Government believes that this act was not committed with the general approval and free will of a people with whom it has lived in complete amity for so many years. It believes that the responsibility rests wholly with the Government of the Orange Free State, acting, not in the interests of the country, but under mischievous

172

influences from without. The British Government, therefore, wishes the people of the Orange Free State to understand that it bears them no ill will and, so far as is compatible with the successful conduct of the war, and the re-establishment of peace in South Africa, it is anxious to preserve them from the evils brought upon them by the wrongful acting of their Government.

I therefore warn all Burghers to desist from any further hostility towards Her Majesty's Government and the troops under my command, and I undertake that any of them, who may so desist and who are found staying in their homes and quietly pursuing their normal occupations, will not be made to suffer in their persons or property on account of their having taken up arms in obedience to the order of their Government. Those, however, who oppose the forces under my command, or furnish the enemy with supplies or information, will be dealt with according to the customs of war.

Requisitions for food, forage, fuel or shelter, made on the authority of the officers in command of Her Majesty's troops, must be at once complied with; but everything will be paid for on the spot, prices being regulated by the local market rates. If the inhabitants of any district refuse to comply with the demands made on them, the supplies will be taken by force, a full receipt being given.

Should any inhabitant of the country consider that he or any member of his household has been unjustly treated by any officer, soldier or civilian attached to the British Army, he should submit his complaint, either personally or in writing, to my Head-Quarters or to the Head-Quarters of the nearest General Officer. Should the complaint on enquiry be substantiated, redress will be given.

Orders have been issued by me, prohibiting soldiers from entering private houses, or molesting the civilian population on any pretext whatever, and every precaution has been taken against injury to property on that [sic] part of any persons belonging to, or connected with, the Army.

ROBERTS, Field Marshal
Commanding-in-Chief, British Forces, South Africa

A further proclamation appears on the same page of the newspaper.

PROCLAMATION
To the Burghers of the Orange Free State

In continuation of the Proclamation which I issued when the British troops under my command entered the Orange Free State, in which I warned all Burghers to desist from any further hostility, and undertook that those of them who might so desist, and were staying in their homes and quietly pursuing their ordinary occupations, would not be made to suffer in their persons or property on account of their having taken up arms in obedience to the order of their Government. I now make known to all Burghers that I have been authorised by the Government of Her Most Gracious Majesty the Queen to offer the following terms to those of them who have been involved in the present war:–

 All burghers who have not taken a prominent part in the policy which has led to the war between Her Majesty and the Orange Free State, or commanded any forces of the Republic, or commandeered or used violence to any British subjects, and who are willing to lay down their arms at once, and to bind themselves by an oath to abstain from further participation in the war, will be given passes to allow them to return to their homes and will not be made prisoners of war, nor will their property be taken from them.

ROBERTS, Field Marshal
Commanding-in-Chief, Her Majesty's Forces in South Africa
Government House, Bloemfontein
15 March 1900

Glossary of Lincolnshire Dialect

ABOUT – almost or nearly, as in 'I'm about better'.

AGAIN or AGAINST – close to, as in 'We're again the Canary Islands'.

BLOT – possibly from ME to destroy, as in 'We gave the enemy a blot'.

BOOM – rumour, as in 'There's a boom going round that ...'

BUG-BLINDING – lime-washing walls to keep down bedbugs, as in 'I hope to be home for the bug-blinding'.

BURN – rumour, similar to a boom.

BUSTER or BLOWOUT – a large meal, as in 'I had a buster today'.

CHAMPION – very well or very good, as in 'I'm going on champion'.

DEFINITE ARTICLES are often left out in Lincolnshire dialect, as in 'Don't give garden up'.

DINNER – the midday meal, as in 'We had fish to our dinner'.

FUDDLE – a booze-up, as in 'We'll have a good fuddle when we get home'.

GIVE IT – punish or reprimand, as in 'I'll give it him when I see him'.

LOOK SHARP – be quick or hurry up, as in 'Look sharp with that job'.

LIE – level, as in 'It looked like a lie but was uphill'.

MUCKY TRICK – a dirty trick, as in 'He played a mucky trick on me'.

PISSMIRE – obsolete term for an ant, 'piss' from the smell of anthill, 'mire' OE for ant.

PLURALS – the s is often left off, as in 'We are four mile off Pretoria'.

SOP – bread and milk, as in 'I've made many a meal of sop'.

SPEC – speculation, as in 'There's a spec about us going home'.

STARVED – very cold, as in 'We were starved on the train'.

STATUTES – annual hiring fairs established by ancient charter, as in 'I hope to be home for the Statutes'.

TEA – the evening meal, as in 'We had coffee and dry bread to our tea'.

TO – for or with, as in the above.

WHILE – until, as in 'We must wait for beer while we come home'.

Bibliography

Amery, L.S., and Williams, B. (eds), *The Times History of the War in South Africa*, Vol. 4, Sampson Low, London, 1906

Branford, Jean, *Dictionary of South African English*, Oxford University Press, Cape Town, 1978

Carrington, C. (ed.), *The Complete Barrack-Room Ballads of Rudyard Kipling*, Methuen, London, 1973

Cousins, Geoffrey, *The Defenders: A History of the British Volunteer*, Frederick Muller, London, 1968

Creed, R., and Coult, A., *Steeltown: The Story of the Men and Women Who Built an Industry*, Hutton Press, Beverley, E. Yorkshire, 1990

Davenport, T.R.H., *South Africa: A Modern History*, Macmillan, London, 1977

Farwell, Byron, *Queen Victoria's Little Wars*, Allen Lane, London, 1973

Goodson, K.W.S., 'Notes on the Genealogy of the Volunteer Force & Territorial Army', manuscript in the County of Lincoln Museum of Lincolnshire Life, Lincoln.

Hart, Col. C.H., *First Volunteer Battalion of the Royal Warwickshire Regiment*, Midland Counties Herald Ltd, 1906

Hull Times – December 1899 to May 1901

Leasor, James, *Rhodes and Barnato: The Premier and the Prancer*, Leo Cooper, London, 1997

Lindsey and Lincolnshire Star – December 1899 to May 1901

Martin, Col. A.C., *The Concentration Camps: Facts, Figures and Fables*, Howard Timmins, Cape Town, 1957

Meintjes, Johannes, *President Paul Kruger*, Cassell, London, 1974

Pakenham, Thomas, *The Boer War*, Weidenfeld & Nicolson, London, 1979

Pakenham, Thomas, *The Boer War*, Illustrated Edition (abridged by J.W. Buchan), Weidenfeld & Nicolson, London, 1993

Price, Richard, *An Imperial War and the British Working Class: Working Class Attitudes and Reactions to the Boer War*, Routledge & Kegan Paul, London, 1972

(Rankin, R.), *A Subaltern's Letters to His Wife*, Longman Green, London, 1901

Reitz, Deneys, *Commando: A Boer Journal of the Boer War*, Faber & Faber, London, 1929

Strachey, Ray, *Millicent Garrett Fawcett*, Murray, London, 1931

Streak, M., *Lord Milner's Immigration Policy for the Transvaal 1899–1905*, Rand Afrikaans University Publications, Series B 1, Johannesburg, 1969

Swaisland, Cecillie, *Servants and Gentlewomen to the Golden Land: The Emigration of Single Women from Britain to Southern Africa 1820–1939*, Berg Press, Oxford, and Providence / University of Natal Press, Pietermaritzburg, 1993

Trevelyan, G.M., *History of England*, 3rd Edition, Longmans, London, 1945

Index